Books, Bodies and Bronzes

T0333848

One out of every seven people in the world today is on the move, voluntarily and involuntarily, within countries and between them. More and more people belong to several communities at once and yet the social contract between state and citizen is still bounded by questions of nationality. Where will the cultural building blocks come from with which we can imagine a different kind of nation, and different kinds of institutions, that better reflect this reality?

This book looks at the potential role of international music competitions, beauty magazines, elite social clubs, overseas university campuses, and religious movements, among others, as potential breeding grounds for the creation of global citizenship.

This book was originally published as a special issue of *Ethnic and Racial Studies*.

Peggy Levitt is Professor of Sociology at Wellesley College, Massachusetts, USA, and the Co-Director of The Transnational Studies Initiative at Harvard University, Cambridge, Massachusetts, USA.

Pál Nyíri is Professor of Global History from an Anthropological Perspective at the Vrije Universiteit, Amsterdam, the Netherlands.

Ethnic and Racial Studies

Series editors: Martin Bulmer, *University of Surrey, UK*, and John Solomos, *University of Warwick, UK*

The journal *Ethnic and Racial Studies* was founded in 1978 by John Stone to provide an international forum for high quality research on race, ethnicity, nationalism and ethnic conflict. At the time the study of race and ethnicity was still a relatively marginal sub-field of sociology, anthropology and political science. In the intervening period the journal has provided a space for the discussion of core theoretical issues, key developments and trends, and for the dissemination of the latest empirical research.

It is now the leading journal in its field and has helped to shape the development of scholarly research agendas. *Ethnic and Racial Studies* attracts submissions from scholars in a diverse range of countries and fields of scholarship, and crosses disciplinary boundaries. It is now available in both printed and electronic form. From 2015 it will publish 15 issues per year, three of which will be dedicated to *Ethnic and Racial Studies Review* offering expert guidance to the latest research through the publication of book reviews, symposia and discussion pieces, including reviews of work in languages other than English.

The *Ethnic and Racial Studies* book series contains a wide range of the journal's special issues. These special issues are an important contribution to the work of the journal, where leading social science academics bring together articles on specific themes and issues that are linked to the broad intellectual concerns of *Ethnic and Racial Studies*. The series editors work closely with the guest editors of the special issues to ensure that they meet the highest quality standards possible. Through publishing these special issues as a series of books, we hope to allow a wider audience of both scholars and students from across the social science disciplines to engage with the work of *Ethnic and Racial Studies*.

Titles in the series include:

The Transnational Political Participation of Immigrants
Edited by Jean-Michel Lafleur and Marco Martiniello

Anthropology of Migration and Multiculturalism
Edited by Steven Vertovec

Books, Bodies and Bronzes

Comparing sites of global
citizenship creation

Edited by
Peggy Levitt and Pál Nyíri

Routledge
Taylor & Francis Group

LONDON AND NEW YORK

ETHNIC
AND
RACIAL
STUDIES

First published 2015
by Routledge

2 Park Square, Milton Park, Abingdon, Oxon OX14 4RN
711 Third Avenue, New York, NY 10017, USA

Routledge is an imprint of the Taylor & Francis Group, an informa business

First issued in paperback 2017

British Library Cataloguing in Publication Data
A catalogue record for this book is available from the British Library

ISBN 13: 978-1-138-88802-9 (hbk)
ISBN 13: 978-1-138-08281-6 (pbk)

Typeset in Times New Roman
by RefineCatch Limited, Bungay, Suffolk

Publisher's Note
The publisher accepts responsibility for any inconsistencies that may have
arisen during the conversion of this book from journal articles to book chapters,
namely the possible inclusion of journal terminology.

Disclaimer
Every effort has been made to contact copyright holders for their permission to
reprint material in this book. The publishers would be grateful to hear from any
copyright holder who is not here acknowledged and will undertake to rectify
any errors or omissions in future editions of this book.

Contents

Citation Information

The chapters in this book were originally published in *Ethnic and Racial Studies*, volume 37, issue 12 (October 2014). When citing this material, please use the original page numbering for each article, as follows:

Chapter 1
Introduction: Books, bodies, and bronzes: comparing sites of global citizenship creation
Peggy Levitt and Pál Nyíri
Ethnic and Racial Studies, volume 37, issue 12 (October 2014)
pp. 2149–2157

Chapter 2
Vogue and the possibility of cosmopolitics: race, health and cosmopolitan engagement in the global beauty industry
Giselinde Kuipers, Yiu Fai Chow and Elise van der Laan
Ethnic and Racial Studies, volume 37, issue 12 (October 2014)
pp. 2158–2175

Chapter 3
Shifting tides of world-making in the UNESCO World Heritage Convention: cosmopolitanisms colliding
Christoph Brumann
Ethnic and Racial Studies, volume 37, issue 12 (October 2014)
pp. 2176–2192

Chapter 4
Cosmopolitan theology: Fethullah Gülen and the making of a 'Golden Generation'
Thijl Sunier
Ethnic and Racial Studies, volume 37, issue 12 (October 2014)
pp. 2193–2208

CITATION INFORMATION

Chapter 5
Globalizing forms of elite sociability: varieties of cosmopolitanism in Paris social clubs
Bruno Cousin and Sébastien Chauvin
Ethnic and Racial Studies, volume 37, issue 12 (October 2014)
pp. 2209–2225

Chapter 6
Pirate cosmopolitics and the transnational consciousness of the entertainment industry
Olga Sezneva
Ethnic and Racial Studies, volume 37, issue 12 (October 2014)
pp. 2226–2242

Chapter 7
Between global citizenship and Qatarization: negotiating Qatar's new knowledge economy within American branch campuses
Neha Vora
Ethnic and Racial Studies, volume 37, issue 12 (October 2014)
pp. 2243–2260

Chapter 8
Tuning in or turning off: performing emotion and building cosmopolitan solidarity in international music competitions
Lisa McCormick
Ethnic and Racial Studies, volume 37, issue 12 (October 2014)
pp. 2261–2280

Please direct any queries you may have about the citations to
clsuk.permissions@cengage.com

Notes on Contributors

Christoph Brumann is Head of the Research Group 'The Global Political Economy of Cultural Heritage' at the Max Planck Institute for Social Anthropology, Halle, Germany; and Honorary Professor of Anthropology, University of Halle-Wittenberg, Germany.

Sébastien Chauvin is Assistant Professor in the Department of Sociology and Anthropology at the University of Amsterdam, the Netherlands.

Yiu Fai Chow is Assistant Professor in the Department of Humanities and Creative Writing at Baptist University, Hong Kong.

Bruno Cousin is Assistant Professor in the Department of Sociology and Anthropology at the University of Lille 1, France.

Giselinde Kuipers is Professor of Cultural Sociology at the University of Amsterdam, the Netherlands.

Peggy Levitt is Professor of Sociology at Wellesley College, Massachusetts, USA, and Co-Director of the Transnational Studies Initiative, Harvard University, Cambridge, Massachusetts, USA.

Lisa McCormick is Assistant Professor in the Department of Sociology at Haverford College, Pennsylvania, USA.

Pál Nyíri is Professor of Global History from an Anthropological Perspective at the Vrije Universiteit, Amsterdam, the Netherlands.

Olga Sezneva is Assistant Professor in the Department of Sociology and Anthropology at the University of Amsterdam, the Netherlands.

Thijl Sunier is Professor of Cultural Anthropology in the Department of Social and Cultural Anthropology at the Vrije Universiteit, Amsterdam, the Netherlands.

Elise van der Laan is a Ph.D. candidate in the Department of Sociology, University of Amsterdam, the Netherlands.

Neha Vora is Assistant Professor in the Department of Anthropology and Sociology at Lafayette College, Easton, Pennsylvania, USA.

INTRODUCTION

Books, bodies, and bronzes: comparing sites of global citizenship creation

Peggy Levitt and Pál Nyíri

This volume explores music competitions, religious movements, fashion magazines, copyright policy and overseas university campuses, among others, as potential sites for the generation and spread of cosmopolitan ideas, competencies and projects. Our contributors focus on how and when that happens, in what combinations, and what difference it makes when aspects of cosmopolitanism are disseminated at music competitions, UNESCO World Heritage sites, or through membership in elite social clubs. They embed the production and dissemination of cosmopolitanism within cultural and institutional contexts, thereby bringing to light not just the classroom, editorial room and stage, but the complex, power-laden set of organizational arrangements that undergird them and the geopolitical context within which they take shape.

While preparing to write the introduction to this special volume, we accidentally stumbled on what was, to us, a new field of study that might be called 'global citizenship education studies'. Our literature review came up with numerous articles, written by education professionals, about how to prepare twenty-first-century students for the twenty-first-century global world (De Oliveira Andreotti, and de Souza 2012). And this research was not just about primary or secondary school students. Many studies focused on the need for university education to include mandatory study abroad programmes, foreign language courses offering more than just Romance languages, and student bodies made up of people from around the world. What drives all these developments is a sense that the world is changing and that everyone, from first graders to college graduates, needs to be prepared to participate in new ways. While the literature tends to focus on

North America, Europe and Australia, 'global citizenship education' is itself a global phenomenon (Lee and Leung 2006).

In the 1930s and 1940s USA in which Peggy Levitt's parents grew up, students took civic courses in which they learned about the workings of government and the importance of active democratic participation. In Eastern Europe, under late state socialism, where Pál Nyíri spent his school years, efforts to mint 'socialist citizens' were no longer much in evidence; rather, schools taught pupils what they had since the times of Rousseau: about the unique qualities of the nations where they were born. In short, an important piece of the curriculum was to teach students how to be good national citizens. And, it would seem, from the plethora of materials that we encountered, that this is still the case, but with a new twist. Now schools, to varying degrees and in different ways in different places, prepare students to be national citizens and competent cosmopolitans at the same time – to be active and loyal to their nations and to be part of the global community at large.

Perhaps educators have taken the lead because children are seen as more malleable than adults. But where do the rest of us learn how to be global citizens? How do people who have been brought up to identify with and perform the rituals of the nation also learn to belong to and feel responsible for the rest of the world?

In this volume, we go beyond schools to explore other potential sites of global citizenship creation. We are both doing research of our own on these topics. Levitt has completed a book about if and how museums around the world see themselves as creating citizens. She asks what it is about the history and culture of particular cities and nations that helps explain why some cultural institutions are so outward looking while others look barely beyond their doors (Levitt 2012, forthcoming). Nyiri is studying young journalists who report for mainland Chinese media from foreign locations. He wants to find out what stories these correspondents want to tell their audiences in China about the world, and whether a cosmopolitan shift is taking place in segments of the Chinese media, thanks to their efforts.

Through this work, we realized that while there is a great deal of research on the multiple meanings of cosmopolitanism, how and where people actually acquire the values and skills that enable them to engage with difference is little understood. In addition to museums and schools, there are multiple sites around the world where the work of creating global citizens may be under way. How that happens, who reaps the benefits and costs, and what difference it makes when cosmopolitan values are evoked at a music competition versus a UNESCO World Heritage site or in a *Vogue* magazine article is the subject of this volume. Our authors embed the dissemination of identities, ideologies and capabilities within institutional contexts. They not only allow us to see the classroom, editorial room and stage, but the complex, power-laden set of organizational arrangements that undergird them and the geopolitical context within which they take shape.

There is a large body of literature on cosmopolitanism in which it has many faces, ranging from a sociocultural condition to a political orientation, set of skills and practices, or a philosophy or world view (Vertovec and Cohen 2002; Breckenridge et al. 2002). Individuals, organizations, nations and international frameworks and conventions acquire cosmopolitan properties or embody cosmopolitan values. But cosmopolitanism is far from neutral (Harvey 2000, 530). The possibility of cosmopolitanism, or the ability to go from aspiration to reality, gets muddled, writes Roxanne Euben (2006, 181), because we do not pay enough attention to 'how history, culture, and power inflect the very meaning and value of "openness" in ways that render it politically suspect or untenable, even to those whose mobility is extensive and exposures to difference multiple'. The universality of cosmopolitan is also under siege because, as Breckenridge and her colleagues write:

> No true universalism can be constructed without recognizing that there is a diversity of universals on which analyses are based, and that these are often in fact quite particular – not universals at all, but rather interpretations devised for particular historical and conceptual situations. (Breckenridge et al. 2002)

But the sense underlying much of this work is that we need to keep trying. If Euro-American cosmopolitanism was born out of colonial, imperial and missionary experiences that brought home an awareness of worlds other than one's own, it does not monopolize the experience (van der Veer 2002). Today's world travellers and high-flying professionals may or may not repeat the same mistakes as their earlier counterparts who embarked upon 'the requisite European grand tour'. And as new networks of economic power emerge out of China, India and the Gulf and leave their footprints around the world, and as more and more mobile non-elites give rise to transnational middle and working classes, frictions and conflicts as well as cosmopolitan sensibilities will undoubtedly arise. While some individuals will cling consciously to Western versions of cosmopolitanism, others will articulate new combinations of the universal and the particular, of what is relative and what is an unconditional good. All, however, have the potential to turn away from the projects of economic domination from which they arise.

In fact, in today's global, interconnected world, many people argue that some kind of cosmopolitanism is a necessity not a choice (Beck 2006). But, warns Craig Calhoun (2008, 110): 'Cosmopolitan theories need to be supplemented by an emphasis on the material conditions and social institutions that make this sort of cosmopolitan inhabitation of the world possible – and much more likely for some than others.' We need to shift, says Bruno Latour (2004, 457), away from the cosmopolitan to cosmopolitics: not just dreaming of a time when people recognize that they inhabit the same world but actually taking on the daunting task of seeing how that 'same world' can be created.

This is the jumping-off point for the contributions in this volume. Rather than resolving normative or definitional debates, our authors instead shed light on how and where the ideas, skills and politics from which cosmopolitanism is constituted get generated and acquired. They tackle this task by unpacking the various threads of the cosmopolitan project. In some cases, our authors describe how and where a set of cosmopolitanism ideas and values are produced. In others, they describe the articulation and spread of a set of practices and competences. They build upon work by Ulf Hannerz (1990, 239), for example, who wrote that cosmopolitanism is a matter of 'competence marked by a personal ability to make one's way into other cultures, through listening, looking, intuiting and reflecting as well as by a built-up skill of maneuvering through systems of meaning' (see also Gilroy 2005; Glick Schiller, Darieva, and Gruner-Domic 2011; Nowicka and Rovisco 2009). A third view of cosmopolitanism includes the next, difficult step of defining and working towards shared political projects. For Saito (2011), for example, the work does not stop at 'cultural omnivorousness' or the willingness to appreciate a wide variety of cultural objects or at 'ethnic tolerance' or the ability to embrace positive attitudes towards ethnic out-groups. Instead, we need to also take on 'cosmopolitics', or the collective task of creating a transnational public and debating global risks as citizens of the world.

Despite its breadth and depth, much of the research on cosmopolitanism does not shed sufficient light on the messy arenas where this kind of meaning making and negotiation actually take place – where the ethos and aspiration, skills and competencies, and political action projects get produced. What kinds of institutions allow people to create relationships with strangers and be open to difference? How do we go beyond ideas and values to create cosmopolitan sensibilities, skills or institutions? When and how do these get translated into political struggles and schemes? What difference does it make when these dynamics take shape in the context of the copyright regimes, religious social movements or overseas university campuses?

That is where bodies, books and bronzes come in.

Outline of the contributions

We see universities, global music festivals, religious communities and world heritage sites as just some potential sites for the creation of cosmopolitans and political projects. Our contributors take stock of the state of the art of this emerging field and allow us to compare how aspects of cosmopolitanism are produced and disseminated in different sectors and institutional arenas.

Christoph Brumann's article on the politics of UNESCO's World Heritage list opens the issue. Adopted in 1972, the UNESCO Convention Concerning the Protection of the World Cultural and Natural Heritage is one of the earliest, and on the face of it, one of the most successful, initiatives explicitly aimed at instilling a 'planetary consciousness' by affirming the existence of a 'shared heritage of humankind'. Whether or not World Heritage is succeeding among the world's population, Brumann argues that it has, at least, produced a body of – mostly Western – 'experts' committed to 'reforming World Heritage – and thus, indirectly, national heritage conceptions around the world – in a more universalist and inclusive way'. Yet, with the economic and political stakes of World Heritage on the rise since the 1990s, these experts have increasingly been overridden by diplomats who, while cosmopolitan in habitus, represent thoroughly national agendas and are more interested in the quid pro quo of negotiating what gets anointed as 'world heritage' than in rethinking concepts and methods of caring for national patrimony.

Bruno Cousin and Sébastien Chauvin study the production of transnational connections, cosmopolitanism and global class consciousness in elite social clubs in Paris. Even at these upper echelons, distinctions are clearly and resoundingly made – between pure social clubs and what get classified as international service clubs for the upper middle class like Rotary International – and between the types of international social capital and connections members gain access to by belonging to these institutions (some deemed more superficial and utilitarian than others). In fact, clubs disagree over the value of international ties per se, triggering a competing metric within the symbolic economy of social capital accumulation. The different cosmopolitanisms that they engender among their members result not only from their different levels of exposure and sensitivity to global interdependence but also from the dynamics of symbolic competition between class fractions. Besides nationality and economic capital, then, access to social capital is key in determining how well individuals can access global resources and status, and in shaping their cosmopolitan representations and practices.

Thijl Sunier takes up the question of whether religion can inspire cosmopolitanism. He studies *Hizmet*, an Islamic movement founded by Fethullah Gülen in Turkey in the 1960s, which has evolved from its initial focus on Turkish nationalism into a global network of chapters and schools promoting a 'civil Islam'. Its goal is to create a new generation of Muslims who live reflexively and responsibly in today's world – a global Islamic doctrine, argues Sunier, with explicitly cosmopolitan underpinnings.

While some have argued that there is a contradiction between the cosmopolitan inclusiveness and universality of Gülen's message and the strong hierarchical structures and the disciplining modes of teaching and training within the movement, Sunier disagrees. These characteristics are two necessary sides of the same coin. Being a responsible Muslim and a responsible citizen in this world are similar qualities. Openness and inclusiveness on the one hand and strong internal discipline and exclusiveness on the other reinforce rather than contradict each other. To be part of the 'Golden Generation' one must successfully combine a virtuous life with an active this-worldly attitude. An analysis of Gülen's cosmopolitan theology and pedagogy and the ways that it is taught and reproduced, Sunier concludes, must take into account the complex relationship between the political-historical and theological roots of the movement, the vastly changing characteristics of the followers, and the particular pedagogies applied in all kinds of educational settings.

Neha Vora's work also looks at the education sector as a potential site of cosmopolitan creation. She studies one example of the growing number of offshore campuses established by US and European universities in Asia and the Middle East. Many of these schools, in fact, sell 'global citizenship creation', offering educational and life experiences designed to deliver on that promise. Critics, however, see them as tools of cultural imperialism which threaten academic freedom or educational compromises in pursuit of profit. In Education City, Qatar, Vora examines how students, particularly non-citizens, negotiate the apparent disjuncture between Qatarization, a policy that structurally favours citizens, and an American-style university system established to promote cosmopolitan 'global citizenship' based on a belief in individualism, meritocracy and multi-culturalism. The structural inequalities inherent in the *kafala* system and Qatarization permeated students' daily lives even as they negotiated new forms of identity and citizenship made possible by liberal and neo-liberal educational models. As in the case of *Hizmet*, rather than a contradiction in terms, Qatari non-liberal state policies and American liberal higher education are intertwined and rely upon each other in ways that reveal much longer entanglements between these seemingly opposed logics of governance and belonging.

Giselinde Kuipers, Elise van der Laan and Yiu Fai Chow look for the possibility of global citizenship in a seemingly unlikely but highly influential segment of the global media: high-end fashion magazines. They study how two moral issues – the promotion of racially diverse standards of beauty and healthy body types – are treated in *Vogue* in China, the Netherlands and the USA. Their analysis reveals that *Vogue* has the potential to contribute to greater openness to human diversity and to limited omnivorousness but that the extent to which it promoted cosmopolitics varied by country. This is in part, these authors say, because of each country's distinct role and location in the transnational cultural field and the different role that *Vogue* plays as an object and initiator of national public debate and civic engagement.

Olga Sezneva studies entertainment industries in which the artists and fans are increasingly global, as is the prevalence of illegal copying and pirating. Rights-holders have turned to law enforcement and consumer education as two complementary strategies for controlling reproduction. Sezneva's paper looks at the interplay between these two ways of regulating global cultural flows and their effect on cosmopolitan social imaginaries. For these strategies to work, she argues, the entertainment industry has to create a bond between producer and consumer that does not normally exist and a 'subject' willing to embrace a particular attitude and self-conduct towards the private ownership of a creative product. But, in their current state, Sezneva argues, policing efforts fall short because they misread cosmopolitanism, failing to recognize that pirating itself can function as a means to its achievement. Copyright in this context appears to economic participants as an obstacle that thwarts their ability to satisfy their desires and enter into certain cultural communities and publics. Through its infringement, consumers gain access to this more cosmopolitan space and the identities with which it is associated.

Finally, Lisa McCormick explores the ways in which international classical music competition are sites of global citizenship creation. Throughout the twentieth century, these events served as platforms where European nations and Cold War superpowers competed against one another for supremacy in the music world. But as more and more aspects of these events become globalized – the musicians participating, the repertoire performed, the frameworks of evaluation, and the expectations of the audience – they imbued competitors and audience members with global values. McCormick focuses on one way that this happens: how emotion as an indicator or metric of value functions to incorporate a wider range of people into the circle of great musicians. The self, she argues, is transformed by the encounter with the other. In the case of performers, the encounter involves musically 'taking the role of the other' in works that are culturally distant. In the case of the audience, the encounter involves labelling as 'authentic' a performance by a musician performing something culturally distant. The audience feels a sense of solidarity with the musician because they recognize the stylistic accuracy and they are moved by its substance and by how sincerely it is enacted. Competitions act as mediators of cosmopolitanism by creating occasions for 'tuning' in; through music, participants are able to synchronize 'inner time' and experience the '"We" which is at the foundation of all possible communication'.

Taken together, the contributions to this special issue document that discursive and moral regimes of global citizenship are at work in both expected and unexpected places. While they typically rely on global infrastructures, they exert their mobilizing power unevenly in different places. While their impact can by no means be taken for granted, they should not be dismissed out of hand as superficial pastimes of the well-to-do. The varied cases presented here demonstrate that cosmopolitan discourses, tastes and competencies both contribute to and detract from cosmopolitan projects in complex ways. Sometimes, as in the social clubs of the French elite, the former fails to engender the latter; at other times, as in the World Heritage regime, at US university campuses in Qatar, or with respect to global intellectual property regime, they do so in ambivalent, reversible or unintended ways, while sometimes turning out to be quite compatible with nationalist stances. Mobility, migration and transnationalism, too, have an ambivalent relationship with cosmopolitics: while they are present as an enabling infrastructure in many of our cases – from the global circulation of UNESCO experts to the regional circulation of Gülen schoolteachers and university students – they do not always engender a greater concern for non-fellow nationals: as the discussion of *Vogue*'s Oriental Beauty demonstrates, the growing institutionalization of particular transnational communities or diasporas can reinforce racialization.

On the whole, the articles suggest that cosmopolitanism remains largely a middle-class pursuit: the poor may have no access to or use for it, and the rich, as Cousin and Chauvin suggest, may distance themselves from it as a strategy of affirming distinction. Indeed, as Sezneva argues, the regimes and institutions that drive it forward, can have the unintended effect of leaving certain segments of the public out. Nor are the middle classes in different places equally receptive to all aspects of cosmopolitanism, as Kuipers and her co-authors show. Even so, our cases reveal the fairly wide variety and reach of such impulses, from Muslim schoolteachers in Central Asia to hip hop fans in the Global South, 'D-buffs' in China, and – perhaps least surprisingly – classical musicians from Eastern Europe. In this range of cases, political and educational institutions serve as vehicles for the spread of aspects of cosmopolitanism nearly as often as do commercial ones.

References

Beck, Ulrich. 2006. *Cosmopolitan Vision*. Cambridge: Polity.

Breckenridge, Carol, Sheldon Pollock, Homi Bhabha, and Dipesh Chakrabarty. 2002. *Cosmopolitanisms*. Durham, NC: Duke University Press.

Calhoun, Craig. 2008. "Cosmopolitanism in the Modern Social Imaginary." *Daedalus* 137 (3): 105–114.

De Oliveira Andreotti, Vanessa, and Lynn Mario T. M. de Souza. 2012. *Postcolonial Perspectives on Global Citizenship Education*. New York: Routledge Press.

Euben, Roxanne Leslie. 2006. *Journeys to the Other Shore: Muslim and Western Travelers in Search of Knowledge*. Princeton, NJ: Princeton University Press.

Gilroy, Paul. 2005. *Postcolonial Melancholia*. New York: Columbia University Press.

Glick Schiller, Nina, Tsypylma Darieva, and Sandra Gruner-Domic. 2011. "Defining Cosmopolitan Sociability in a Transnational Age." *Ethnic and Racial Studies* 34 (3): 399–418. doi:10.1080/01419870.2011.533781.

Hannerz, Ulf. 1990. "Transnational Connections: Culture, People, Places." In *Global Culture: Nationalism, Globalization and Modernity*, edited by Mike Featherstone, 237–251. London: Sage.

Harvey, David. 2000. *Spaces of Hope*. Berkeley: University of California Press.

Latour, Bruno. 2004. "Whose Cosmos, Which Cosmopolitics? Comments on the Peace Terms of Ulrich Beck." *Common Knowledge* 10 (3): 450–462. doi:10.1215/0961754X-10-3-450.

Lee, Wing On, and Sai Wing Leung. 2006. "Global Citizenship Education in Hong Kong and Shanghai Secondary Schools: Ideals, Realities and Expectations." *Citizenship Teaching and Learning* 2 (3). http://www.citized.info/pdf/ejournal/Vol%202%20Number%202/024.pdf.

Levitt, Peggy. 2012. "The Bog and the Beast: Museums, the Nation, and the World." *Ethnologia Scandinavica* 22: 29–49.

Levitt, Peggy. forthcoming. *The Bog and the Beast: Putting, the Nation, and the World on Display*. Berkeley and Los Angels: University of California Press.

Nowicka, Magdalena, and Maria Rovisco. 2009. *Making Sense of Cosmopolitanism*. Burlington: Ashgate.

Saito, Hiro. 2011. "An Actor-Network Theory of Cosmopolitanism." *Sociological Theory* 29 (2): 124–150.

van der Veer, Peter. 2002. "Colonial Cosmopolitanism." In *Conceiving Cosmopolitanism: Theory, Context and Practice*, edited by Steven Vertovec and Robin Cohen, 165–179. Oxford: Oxford University Press.

Vertovec, Steven, and Robin Cohen. 1996. *Migration, Diasporas and Transnationalism*. Cheltenham, UK: Edward Elgar.

Vertovec, Steven, and Robin Cohen, eds. 2002. *Conceiving Cosmopolitanism: Theory, Context and Practice*, Oxford: Oxford University Press.

Vogue and the possibility of cosmopolitics: race, health and cosmopolitan engagement in the global beauty industry

Giselinde Kuipers, Yiu Fai Chow and Elise van der Laan

This article explores the possibility of cosmopolitics, using the global magazine franchise *Vogue* as our starting point. Drawing on Saito's conceptualizations of cosmopolitanism, we investigate whether *Vogue* promotes cosmopolitan engagement, which we define as promotion of human diversity, cultural omnivorousness and cosmopolitics. Our analysis focuses on racial diversity and health, two moral issues recently addressed by *Vogue* itself. We present a content analysis of *Vogue* and media coverage of *Vogue* in China, the Netherlands and the USA. We conclude that *Vogue*, because of its global basis, high status and reliance on visual materials, has the potential to address and unite transnational publics around global issues. However, the success of such attempts depends on local cultural and institutional contexts and the role of local actors, who may adopt, but also reframe or ignore, attempts to promote cosmopolitan engagement.

Introduction: cosmopolitics in the beauty industry?

Cosmopolitanism is said to be the corollary of globalization: increasing contact with 'otherness' may lead to tolerance and openness to new cultures, tastes and styles (Beck 2002; Delanty 2009). Sociologists, like philosophers before, often describe cosmopolitanism as a personal disposition. However, cosmopolitanism implies a normative engagement with global issues that extends beyond individual moods and motivations (Calhoun 2002). Saito (2011) specifies three dimensions of cosmopolitanism: *tolerance* – openness towards 'human others' – and cultural *omnivorousness* – openness to diverse styles and tastes – fosters the creation of a transnational public sphere where people 'debate global risks and work out collective solutions – to engage in *"cosmopolitics"'* (Saito 2011, 125, emphasis added).

This step towards cosmopolitics moves cosmopolitanism from individual disposition to collective engagement. Tolerance and omnivorousness may result from individual life experiences, although they are often cultivated by institutions like schools, media, museums and other cosmopolitan educators (Levitt and Nyíri, forthcoming). Cosmopolitics, however, requires transnational institutions to spark and shape engagement, and to mobilize publics across national borders. Moreover, debates between 'citizens of the world' (Saito 2011, 130) need transnational arenas, media and intermediaries to facilitate exchange. The question then arises: what institutions can reach, create and potentially unite transnational publics, around what sort of issues? How, where and between whom would a transnational debate unfold? In other words: how does cosmopolitanism become cosmopolitics?

We explore the possibility of cosmopolitics in an institution that may seem unlikely: *Vogue* magazine. *Vogue* has nineteen editions in the Americas, Europe, Asia and Australia, and claims an average circulation of 11.3 million and a monthly online audience of 1.6 million.[1] Because of *Vogue*'s high status in international fashion and media, what gets featured in *Vogue* often 'trickles down' to media around the world. *Vogue* is therefore a global institution that potentially reaches transnational audiences. However, like the entire fashion and beauty industry, it is not exactly known for its political engagement. So: why look for cosmopolitics in *Vogue*?

Vogue has recently launched initiatives that addressed global moral issues and actively speak to transnational publics. In 2008, *Vogue Italia* published *The Black Issue, which* exclusively featured models of African descent. In 2012, editors of all nineteen editions signed the *Vogue* Health Initiative that pledged not to work with underage models and to ensure healthy working conditions for models. These initiatives received global attention. *Vogue*'s global prestige and its reliance on visual materials allowed for smooth diffusion across linguistic and cultural boundaries.

This article takes these attempts at transnational political engagement as the starting point for an exploration of the possibilities and limitations of cosmopolitics. *Vogue* is strategic case to study this because of its high status, global reach and recent normative turn. Scholars, politicians and policy-makers increasingly identify entertainment media as breeding grounds for political engagement. They reach large audiences, including audiences not otherwise interested in politics. The 'entertainization' of politics has broadened the scope of politics to include topics traditionally seen as part of the private or female sphere, like health, lifestyle, body and beauty (vanZoonen 2005). Moreover, political engagement increasingly revolves around consumer issues (Johnston and Taylor 2008; Soper 2007). Consumption is a main source of identity in the global ecumene. Magazines like

Vogue address their readers as cosmopolitan consumers of global brands and trends. Their attempts to cultivate transnational allegiances may become a site for cosmopolitan identification and engagement.

The emergence of cosmopolitics may result from top-down interventions, but also from dissent and protest from below. *Vogue*'s recent normative turn was motivated by ongoing critiques of the fashion world. *Vogue*, therefore, is not only a potential creator or facilitator of cosmopolitics, but also a focal point for debate about issues related to beauty, health and race, and possibly for political engagement *against* the fashion and beauty industry.

Our analysis focuses on two normative issues emphasized by *Vogue*: racial diversity and health.[2] We look at coverage of these themes in *Vogue* and public debates surrounding *Vogue* in China, the USA and the Netherlands. Guided by Saito's three dimensions of cosmopolitanism, we explore to what extent *Vogue* embodies or promotes: (1) tolerance, particularly regarding racial diversity; (2) omnivorousness or openness towards diverse styles and tastes; and (3) cosmopolitics. Since political engagement only translates into cosmopolitics when it resonates among wider publics, we also analyse responses: how is *Vogue*'s engagement with these issues taken up and interpreted in the public domain? Finally, more speculatively, we try to establish whether *Vogue*'s interventions foster cosmopolitics. We define cosmopolitics as transnational normative engagement with global issues of broad concern, addressing not specific groups but 'citizens of the world'.

These questions are a starting point for an exploratory analysis of a topic that is the subject of much theorizing, but little actual research: cosmopolitanism. Rather than provide definitive answers, we aim to produce tentative generalizations and generate new hypotheses about the possibility of cosmopolitics on the basis of a comparative empirical case study. Our analysis suggests that *Vogue*, because of its global basis, high status and reliance on visual materials, has the potential to address and unite transnational publics around global issues like racial diversity and healthy body size. However, the success of such attempts depends on local cultural and institutional contexts and the role of local actors, who may adopt, but also reframe or ignore, attempts to promote cosmopolitan engagement.

Vogue in the global fashion field

Vogue is generally considered the world's most influential fashion magazine (Oliva and Angeletto 2006; Godart and Mears 2009). Founded in the USA, *Vogue* now has nineteen (women's) editions around the globe. Although publisher Condé Nast does not own all local editions, the brand identity is carefully controlled. Each edition cultivates a certain local flavour, but all editions aim to make readers feel connected with global high fashion: the runways of Milan, New York and Tokyo; the glamour and adventure of global cities, tropical beaches and the international jet set.

Vogue sets the standard in global fashion for anything from models' looks and new fashion trends to styles in photography, styling and writing. However, it rarely uses its power for moral or political interventions. The 'edgy', avant-garde aesthetics of high fashion is not easily reconciled with a normative stance. Moreover, normative statements may be commercially unattractive because they spoil the mood of hedonism and luxury consumption.

The international fashion and beauty industry is widely criticized for the diffusion of unrealistic and unhealthy body standards; exploitation of (young) models; and the reproduction of racial and ethnic stereotypes. Some brands have responded to this critique. Dove Cosmetics launched an international campaign portraying 'real women' of diverse body sizes and ethnic backgrounds (Johnston and Taylor 2008). However, high fashion generally ignored its critics. What interests us is not why *Vogue* has taken up these critiques, or why so late, but rather: *how* have they addressed them and to what effect? What happens when *Vogue* addresses its readership in an ethical or moral register?

Method and data

This article analyses cosmopolitan engagement in *Vogue*, and responses to this, in the USA, China and the Netherlands. This comparison allows us to trace transnational flows of images and ideas, and connect them with relations and positions in the transnational cultural field of fashion and beauty. The USA, the country of origin of *Vogue*, occupies a powerful central position in this field. China and the Netherlands represent two versions of 'periphery'. China is a global economic and political power and an important manufacturer of fashion. However, for new or prestigious styles, brands, trends and models, the Chinese generally look to global centres abroad. The Netherlands is small and linked with nearby fashion centres like Paris and London through production (models, designers) and consumption. Its position is best summarized as 'suburban' in relation to global fashion: well connected but fundamentally dependent. Our comparison does not attempt to contrast national characteristics or institutional constellations. Instead, following Shih (2013), we understand 'comparison as relation': distinctive relations link these three countries in the fashion and beauty world system.

First, we did an explorative content analysis of the 2012 editions of American, Chinese and Dutch *Vogue* to assess the prominence and framing (cf. deVreese 2005) of issues of health and race. We investigated

13

specifically whether the framing of these themes promoted openness to diversity, omnivorousness and/or cosmopolitics. This phase was deliberately open-ended to allow us to discover cosmopolitics in unexpected shapes and places.

Second, we did a content analysis of the national press in these countries from 2008 to 2012. For the USA and the Netherlands, we used LexisNexis, which includes a wide selection of online and offline news media. For China, we used three archives of Chinese periodicals and newspapers: Wisenet, *Zhongguo Qikanwang* and *Zhongguo Baozhi Ziyuan Qunwen Shujuku*.[3] These databases provide a good starting point for understanding public debates because they cover a wide range of media, audiences and genres, including online sources. To gauge the presence and framing of racial diversity we searched 'Vogue' combined with 'Vogue Black'; 'Black Issue'; 'African-American'; 'ethnic'; 'diversity'; 'colored'; 'race'; 'Chinese'; 'oriental'. For health, we looked for 'Vogue' and 'Health Initiative'; 'health'; 'thin models'; 'weight'; 'body size' (and Dutch and Chinese equivalents). While we did not systematically measure coding reliability, we jointly discussed our data and interpretations.

This study is not a classical comparative analysis: our goal is not to explain differences and similarities between China, the Netherlands and the USA. Looking for global phenomena, we expect similar themes and treatments of these themes across countries. Therefore, we have pooled our findings, analysing them as a set to compare the conditions under which cosmopolitics may emerge.

Black beauty and Oriental beauty: *Vogue* and racial diversity

The fashion and beauty industry has often been critiqued for its racial politics. Models around the world are white, often blue-eyed and blonde (Frith et al. 2005), embodying Western middle-class ideals of slim, pale beauty (Mears 2011).

In July 2008, *Vogue Italia*, the most avant-garde of all *Vogue* editions, published *The Black Issue*, which exclusively featured models of African descent photographed by star photographer Stephen Meisel.[4] It contained photo shoots with black celebrities and top models, a critical article (in Italian) about the portrayal of women of colour, and artistic-looking collages of stereotypical images of black women. Afterwards, *Vogue Italia* published an English-Italian website dedicated to 'Black Beauty' that explicitly targets a global audience.

The Black Issue is a cause célèbre in the fashion world. It sold very well, in and outside Italy (Watson 2008), and perfectly matched the high fashion aesthetic: stylized, glamorous, yet experimental and provocative, with Naomi Campbell's bare breasts, cut-up images of offensive stereotypes, and edgy models in awkward poses. In itself, the decision to use

14

black models in Italy, a country that is neither very racially mixed nor race-conscious, was provocative. The editor's introduction, critical articles and art works communicated the issue's political intent.

The Black Issue/Vogue Black website is our first case for exploring the possibility of cosmopolitics in *Vogue*. It champions racial diversity and its attempt to broaden the *Vogue* aesthetics by including dark-skinned models promotes omnivorousness. It takes a normative stance on an issue that, in Italy, is not local, and concerns a social category that is globally disadvantaged (although the individuals represented are privileged). It reached transnational publics. In addition to the international sales success, *The Black Issue/Vogue* Black website received press coverage in all three of our countries. We located twenty-nine articles in the USA, three articles in China and two in the Netherlands. Dutch and Chinese articles were neutral and factual. For instance, *Xinmin Wanbao* (November 14, 2008) discussed *The Black Issue* in conjunction with Michelle Obama's rise as a style icon.[5]

In the American media, the coverage was extensive, opinionated and typically favourable. *The Black Issue* was discussed in *Ebony* magazine, in blogs like *Gawker*, in popular, regional newspapers (*The Daily Oklahoman*) and in elite newspapers (*The New York Times*). *The Washington Post* published a long, complimentary profile of *Vogue Italia*'s editor:

> Franca Sozzani, the editor of *Vogue Italia*, has taken the lead on one of the most fraught topics in her industry: diversity. She did so in reaction to runways that, in the past few years, had turned strikingly homogenous as a steady stream of pin-thin, white models – most hailing from Eastern Europe – began to dominate the catwalks of New York and Europe. The result of the whitewashed runways meant that the women being funneled into magazines, cosmetics contracts and ultimately into our popular consciousness as archetypes of the feminine ideal were overwhelmingly white and often emaciated. … Under the prestigious banner of *Vogue Italia*, Sozzani now celebrates black and brown women, fat girls and obese ones, too. (*The Washington Post*, November 28, 2010)

New York-based blog Fashiontribe hailed *The Black Issue* as a 'coveted' artefact in the fashion world:

> The fabulous Haute Concept managed to snag a few extra copies of the coveted issue, which, as they note, has been harder to locate than a hooker in a church. To win one, snap a pic of yourself holding a sign that says I'm Haute, email it into them pronto. (Scott 2008)

But it also received praise from the opposite end of the media landscape, feminist blog Jezebel:

> While perhaps some may be upset that it took a "stunt" like this to throw a spotlight on the issue of the lack of diversity in magazines and runways, it's

actually a beautiful souvenir, a keepsake to remember these troubled times.
A protest song in photograph form. Never has the racism issue looked quite
so stunning. (Stewart 2008)

In the USA, *The Black Issue/Vogue* Black resonated with concerns about
race and representation. It coincided with a surge of interest in the politics
of race after the election of Barack Obama. Praise for *Vogue* Black was
sometimes accompanied by snarky remarks at American *Vogue*. While
American *Vogue* had images of women of colour in every 2012 issue
(including cover images of Rihanna, Jennifer Lopez and Serena Williams),
our analysis shows that racial diversity is never explicitly addressed. The
American press embraced the Italian plea for diversity that they apparently
missed in American *Vogue*.

Dutch coverage of *Vogue* Black was limited and neutral – in marked
contrast, as we shall see, with another Sozzani initiative, *Vogue Curvy*.
Despite the presence of a significant non-white community in the
Netherlands, diversity is generally framed in cultural rather than racial
terms (Uitermark 2012). Dutch *Vogue* shows limited racial diversity.
Although the first issue featured Sudanese-British model Alek Wek, most
2012 issues feature no women (or men) of colour, and the issue of race/
ethnicity was never addressed.

In China, attention to *Vogue* Black was rare as well. However, another
racial issue was prominent in the Chinese press and *Vogue China*: Chinese
beauty. Over the years, Chinese *Vogue* has promoted Oriental beauty. We
found seven cover stories with related themes since Chinese *Vogue*'s
inauguration in 2005. In September 2010, *Vogue China* presented its
Oriental Beauty issue. The cover showed six Chinese models wearing
Chinese designer Alexander Wang, photographed by star photographers
Van Lamsweerde and Matadin. The lead article claims: 'Oriental beauty is
no longer an exotic accessory to the Western world.'[6] The article cites a
range of Chinese female celebrities including Chinese American journalist
Connie Chung, Chinese American politician Elaine Chao and Chinese
Australian chef Kylie Kwong. 'These Chinese women didn't only
contribute to their own fields, but also propagate Chinese culture to
different corners of the world.' The lead article focuses more on 'Oriental'
than on beauty, since these women do not owe their celebrity (primarily) to
their looks. However, the cover and the remainder of the issue celebrates
Oriental beauty by showing pretty, anonymous Asian models.

Like *Vogue* Black, the Oriental Beauty frame promotes a broadening of
representation of beauty beyond white or Western-dominated standards. Its
showcasing of Chinese designers and successful Chinese women can be
seen as promoting omnivorousness, showing a greater variety of styles and
people than commonly present in *Vogue*. However, it moves away from
the focus on physical beauty of *Vogue* Black, and uses beauty to appeal
specifically to all women of Chinese descent. While *Vogue* Black

ostentatiously targets global audiences, Oriental Beauty addresses Chinese audiences – including 'overseas Chinese'. Thus, in a manner reminiscent of Chow's (2011) analysis of Miss China Europe, Chinese beauty is incorporated into the transnational cultural politics of 'Chineseness'. The plea for Chinese beauty aims to muster national and/or racial allegiances in the wake of the 'Rise of China'. The Chinese word used to denote 'race' – *minzu* – also means 'nation' and 'ethnicity' (Dikötter 2003). Thus, the Oriental Beauty issue does not really promote racial diversity. Instead, it becomes part of a 'Chineseness' project that conflates race, ethnicity and nation.

The Oriental Beauty issue and Chinese *Vogue*'s campaign for Chinese beauty received little mention in the international press. In our sample, only US-based *Business Insider* (May 15, 2012) discussed it, focusing on the global success of Asian models: 'Meet 10 Asian models who are making waves in the fashion industry.' Interestingly, American and Dutch accounts of *Vogue China* were diametrically opposed to this Oriental Beauty frame. They revolved around a single frame, captured in a *Washington Post* headline: 'Foreign models flock to China, which is increasingly embracing a Western fashion aesthetic.' The article notes: 'China's Next Top Model may well be a blue-eyed Canadian blonde named Nicole (*Washington Post*, December 26, 2009).'

Both the promotion of black and Oriental beauty and this rather hegemonic reporting on Chinese *Vogue* highlight the political dimension of beauty and race. While Dutch and American *Vogue* downplay this, *Vogue* Black and Chinese *Vogue* successfully challenge the exclusionary politics of Western-oriented beauty standards. This strategy of showcasing 'racial beauty' manages to speak to transnational audiences because the images easily transcend national and linguistic boundaries. Moreover, it connects the personal – beauty – with the political, potentially mobilizing new publics for an old cause. When it fails as a political statement, showcasing glamorous 'racial beauty' may still work as an aesthetic statement. Finally, it works because brand and cause reinforce each other. As long as it is 'fabulous', the touting of racial beauty does not imperil *Vogue*'s commercial interests. At the same time, the *Vogue* brand gives glamour to the issue of diversity and equal representation.

Vogue Black underlines the potential for beauty as a route to cosmopolitics: it speaks to transnational audiences, both addressing and drawing attention to globally excluded groups. While the Oriental Beauty frame is also explicitly transnational, this transnationalism seems partisan rather than cosmopolitan. The lack of international coverage of the Oriental Beauty issue attests to this. Thus, while both frames highlight the transnational political dimension of beauty, only *Vogue* Black makes a credible effort at cosmopolitics as we define it. While it does not find appreciative audiences everywhere, it reaches transnational audiences and promotes diversity of style (omnivorousness) and race (human diversity), in a manner that departs rather dramatically from common standards in home country Italy and the fashion world. The Oriental Beauty frame, on the other hand, fails to become cosmopolitical: it promotes Chinese styles, celebrities and models to a (transnational) Chinese audience. Thus, rather than advocating tolerance and openness to diversity, it promotes transnational identity politics.

The Health Initiative: *Vogue* and the framings of health

Our second case study is the *Vogue* Health Initiative (HI): a statement published simultaneously in all June 2012 editions of the magazine. It consists of a six-point manifesto in which the editors vow: (1) not to work with models who are under sixteen or 'appear to have an eating disorder'; (2) ask agents and casting directors not to send or hire models under sixteen; (3) promote industry-wide awareness of health issues; (4) encourage healthy backstage conditions; (5) 'encourage designers to consider the consequences of unrealistically small sample sizes of their clothing'; and (6) 'we will be ambassadors for the message of a healthy body image'.

The HI builds on the 2007 Health Initiative from the Council of Fashion Designers of America (CFDA) and the British Fashion Council. It is also inspired by *Vogue* Curvy – a subsidiary of *Vogue Italia*, featuring 'curvy' models and celebrities. While not all elements of the HI are equally measurable or concrete, together they entail considerable commitment. Moreover, the HI affects all issues and activities of *Vogue*, around the world, from the moment of publication. The HI is therefore best understood as an initiative promoting corporate social responsibility: 'a continuing commitment by an organization to behave ethically and contribute to economic development, while also improving the quality of life of its employees..., the local community, and society at large' (Lindgreen and Swaen 2010, 3).

The HI is a response to ongoing criticisms of global fashion. The vast majority of the world's population is regularly exposed to images of the thin and young models favoured in the fashion field. Few people meet these standards, but many try to emulate them. In terms of the dimensions of cosmopolitanism, the HI makes a brave attempt at cosmopolitics: it tries to unite a transnational public around a global issue. The simultaneous launch in all nineteen issues underlines the global dimension – and the strength of a transnational institution like *Vogue*. However, the HI comes up short with respect to other dimensions of cosmopolitanism: it does not necessarily promote openness to diversity or stylistic omnivorousness.

Turning to our data, it is striking how differently the HI is framed in different editions. The cover of the American edition shows three American athletes, two female (one black) and one male. The editorial introduction, a forceful defence of the HI, shows a picture of Doutzen Kroes, who was:

> rejected in the past for not conforming to some inconceivable and offensive idea of how she should look and what she should weigh. For the record, the five-foot-nine Dutch model wears a 4. Yet to some in fashion, she is far too curvaceous. To everyone else, Kroes looks like exactly what she is – a particularly glowing and radiant example of gorgeousness. (Wintour 2012)

The editorial notes various health challenges to the fashion world and the world at large, including anorexia and 'obesity levels… rocketing upward'.

In all 2012 issues of American *Vogue*, health is a prominent theme. Health is often framed in terms of weight and body size, for instance in articles about 'embracing the voluptuous woman' in fashion (Yaeger 2012) or getting a 'rounder and curvier silhouette' (DeSanctis 2012). A much-criticized article in April 2012 gave a first-person account of a woman's struggle with her young daughter's obesity. Both the article and the critiques link fashion, health and body size in a single media frame. Thus, health is linked with openness to human diversity, although in a broader sense than Saito's ethnic/racial definition: acceptance of diverse body types. In American *Vogue*, therefore, the HI encompasses all three dimensions of cosmopolitanism.

In the Netherlands, by contrast, the HI's presentation was understated: a translation of the HI, the same image of Kroes and a commentary in the Editor's Letter. The issue features short pieces on 'beauty ideals' by several writers, none of which takes a particularly clear stance, and a photo shoot with a model cycling in sports gear. The cover shows a slim, pale model and makes no mention of the HI. As *Vogue*'s project coordinator told us, this was the first year of Dutch *Vogue*, so they felt no need to change much.[7] In general, health and body size are less thematized in Dutch *Vogue*. As a new franchise, Dutch *Vogue* was more concerned with winning over Dutch audiences than with broadening its politics of representation.

The Chinese June issue, finally, has the Chinese version of the HI manifesto. The cover shows (again) Doutzen Kroes, announcing, in English, 'Healthy living'. The Editor's Letter frames the HI, remarkably, in terms of 'simple living'. Editor Angelica Cheung reflects on her daily life, ending with a plea for a simple, healthy lifestyle: controlling her online time, donating unused clothes to charities, buying organic food and making home-cooked meals instead of buying takeaway. She writes: 'In today's materialistically rich society, the quality life we pursue should be about "better", not "more!" I decided to take action, to simplify life.'[8] The entire issue is similarly framed: simplicity is health, discussing issues like 'how to spend 30 days in 15 outfits'. Later in 2012, Chinese *Vogue* was the first to break the HI, violating its one measureable element. The August issue featured Ondria Hardin, a fifteen-year-old white American model. In China, health is not self-evidently linked with either body size or underage models. Consequently, the moral message of the HI becomes more individualized and less cosmopolitan.

The HI received considerable media coverage in all three countries. In the USA, Lexis-Nexis finds fifty-three mentions in 2012, mainly in style magazines and critical blogs, but also in elite and popular newspapers (*The New York Times, New York Observer, Pittsburgh Post-Gazette*) and business publications (*International Business Times*). American coverage of the HI is best summarized as cautiously positive. Jezebel called it 'potentially pretty ground-breaking' (Sauers 2012) and Fashionista wrote:

> While the language in the new manifesto... is a bit noncommittal at times, the new initiative is without a doubt a step in the right direction – and it should make a big impact on the kind of models and editorials we see in the magazines. (Phelan 2012)

The *Christian Science Monitor* (May 4, 2012), in an appreciative article, quotes a model: 'Every model and every magazine looks up to them [*Vogue*] as the standard. I can only imagine this will be a solid step in a direction that will benefit models for generations to come.' However, some media seem sceptical. *The New York Times* (May 3, 2012) calls the initiative 'unusual in that the magazines are wading into a controversial issue'.

The wide American coverage is related to the prominence of American media discourses on health, modelling, thinness and beauty standards. Our LexisNexis search of 'Vogue', 'thin' and 'health' yielded many critical mentions of *Vogue*, couched in a larger critical discourse on the fashion world's unhealthy beauty standards. American media also praised *Vogue Italia*'s Curvy website, which like *Vogue* Black presents a variety of body shapes and sizes, with the same avant-garde aesthetic.

After the cautiously positive reception, American media continued to check *Vogue*'s compliance with its pledge. Fashionista investigates all nineteen editions, asking: 'So did Vogue's Health Initiative actually change anything?' (Kruspe 2012). Blisstree reports: 'Surprise! Vogues Health Initiative covers aren't so body positive' (Rognlin 2012). American media also report critically about a smoking model in the German HI issue: 'She may not be an underage underweight model and she may not have been made-up or retouched, but she's doing one of the most unhealthy things you can do' (Mau 2012).The breach of the HI by *Vogue China* was widely reported in general and fashion media. American media appear to cast themselves in the role of watchdog of the fashion industry. American coverage also played a central role in making the Chinese violation of the HI an international scandal.

In the Netherlands, we found five newspaper articles covering the HI when it was launched. Four were appreciative, but the conservative Calvinist *Nederlands Dagblad* (May 5, 2012) published a mocking entry in the daily limerick contest. The pledge was mentioned twice later in 2012, notably in a critical article in *NRC Handelsblad* (January 10, 2012) about (failing) attempts to regulate the modelling business. This article is the only Dutch source reporting Chinese *Vogue*'s breaking the pledge.

In the Netherlands, like the USA, we found a widespread critical media discourse on the beauty industry: searches for combinations of 'Vogue', 'thin' and 'models' yielded dozens of hits connecting the modelling industry with eating disorders, body dissatisfaction and exploitation of young women. *Vogue* Curvy (unlike *Vogue* Black) was covered in various newspapers. *NRC Next* (the younger subsidiary of prestigious *NRC Handelsblad*) (March 18, 2010) approvingly notes that the models in Curvy are smiling, in contrast with their 'emaciated, pale, heroin chic' sisters: 'Finally an alternative for the army of stick insects presenting itself to us year after year in magazines and advertising.' However, their conclusion is critical: 'If *Vogue Italia* were consistent, it would rename itself *Vogue Italia* White and Skinny. This is what remains when curvy and black are crossed out.'

In Dutch media, *Vogue* functions as a symbol for the beauty standards of high fashion: these standards, like *Vogue* itself, are presented as non-Dutch. In a recurring trope, Dutch models who made it abroad – with their appearance in *Vogue* as proof of their success – are described as too 'down-to-earth' for the international fashion world. Popular daily *Algemeen Dagblad* (November 21, 2012, italicized is English in original, in an otherwise Dutch text) cites a Dutch celebrity celebrating the anniversary of her personality magazine *LINDA*: 'In Vogue they have a different thin top model every month… At LINDA they do it with one *middle aged, plus size model*.' To inhabitants of a semi-peripheral nation like the Netherlands, global brands do not necessarily foster belonging. Instead, they can be used to demarcate local identity. This Dutch framing of *Vogue* as 'Other' may explain why the HI in the Netherlands received less coverage than in the USA, despite the shared critical discourse. Consequently, the HI is less likely to foster cosmopolitanism or cosmopolitics in the Dutch context.

In China, finally, the three databases yielded seven reports on the HI. All were published in May 2012 in the wake of the HI, mostly in national and local newspapers, ranging from *Guoji Caijing Ribao* (Chinese edition of *International Business Times*), *Jiafang* (liberation) *Daily* (generally considered part of the party propaganda apparatus) to *Huanjing Yu Shenghuo*, an environment and lifestyle magazine. These articles, like their American and Dutch counterparts, showed appreciation of the HI and *Vogue*'s role in the campaign against thin and underage models. In that sense, they formed a continuation of a series of Chinese media reports concerning body image, femininity and health issues in connection to fashion models.

The HI received positive – though modest – reception in the Chinese print media. However, these reports of the HI were not embedded in wider critical media discourses on the beauty industry. Moreover, they were framed as part of the global fashion industries, without specific reference to the Chinese context. For instance, *Guoji Caijing Ribao* (May 7, 2012) describes the HI as 'progress', but it speaks of 'girls' in general, commenting: 'In the pursuit of model-like bodies, girls are harming their own health, succumbing to eating disorders and even sacrificing their lives.' Thus, like the Dutch coverage, it appears to place the HI outside the national context, removing much of its potential for or appeal to cosmopolitical engagement.

A sceptical report was published, interestingly, by the official English-language *China Daily* (May 7, 2012). Questioning the sincerity of the HI, it asked: '*Vogue* vow more hype than health?' This article was produced by the Associated Press and published in English-language newspapers around the world. Possibly, *China Daily*, serving as 'a unique window into China by giving the Chinese perspective on the major financial, political and social issues',[9] expects its readership to be attuned to Western critiques of the fashion world. Alternatively, *The China Daily* could feel the need to show the (English-speaking) world its support for the more orthodox party line of suspecting a Western initiative.

The Chinese breach of the HI received little attention. In 2012 alone, London Olympics, Samsung and Apple were reported to employ Chinese underage workers. Thus, it is unsurprising that this particular breach received scant media attention in China. *Vogue China*'s editor Angelica Cheung's apology, however, was widely reported on Chinese online news portals.[10] Cheung explained that the photos were taken before the HI and used by accident. She accepted responsibility and pledged never to commit the same error again. Meanwhile, the chairman of Vogue International, Jonathan Newhouse, was quoted as apologizing publically, emphasizing that the error took place 'in China'. This seems intended to piggyback onto the general assumption that China is a nation where child labour and other abuses of labour rights occur regularly. By framing the breach as localized and confined to China, the main ethical thrust of the HI could remain intact. However, this particular framing stresses a distinction between the Chinese situation and *Vogue*'s cosmopolitan stance, which is unlikely to appeal to Chinese readers' cosmopolitan inclinations.

Discussion and conclusion

This article explored the possibility of cosmopolitics, using the global magazine franchise *Vogue* as our starting point. We focused on two moral issues identified by *Vogue* itself: the promotion of racially diverse standards of beauty and of 'the message of a healthy body image'. To gauge the transnational dynamics of cosmopolitical engagement, we looked at three countries with different positions in the transnational fashion field.

Drawing on Saito's work on cosmopolitanism, we asked three questions. To what extent does *Vogue* promote cosmopolitanism, defined as openness to human diversity, omnivorousness and cosmopolitics? To what extent are *Vogue*'s attempts at cosmopolitan engagement taken up in public debates? Do they foster cosmopolitics: do they address issues faced by people around the world? These questions formed the starting point for our exploratory analysis. We aimed to produce tentative generalizations and generate new questions and hypotheses about the possibility of cosmopolitics.

Our analysis showed that *Vogue* has the potential to contribute to greater openness to human diversity. The *Vogue* Black and Oriental Beauty frames promote tolerance by embracing non-white beauty. The framing of health in American *Vogue*, as openness to diverse body types, also touts human diversity. While not usually included in discussions of cosmopolitanism (Saito 2011), acceptance of physical variation implies general tolerance that surpasses common definitions focusing on ethnic or racial diversity. The Dutch and Chinese framings of health are less cosmopolitan by this standard.

Pleas for a broader understanding of human beauty, to include diverse body sizes and racial types, signify broader and more inclusive tastes. Also, the aesthetic style of *Vogue* is based on innovation, provocation and thus the expansion of styles and tastes. *Vogue* can therefore be said to promote omnivorousness among its readers. However, the *Vogue* aesthetic is also highly exclusive: *Vogue* models conform to specific standards of rarefied beauty. Even non-white and 'curvy' models are young, stunning, well proportioned, with small (stereotypically non-African) noses and large (stereotypically non-Asian) eyes. Thus, *Vogue*'s omnivorousness has clear limits.

To what extent does *Vogue* promote cosmopolitics? Looking at the content of *Vogue*, we concluded that *Vogue* Black and the American version of the HI represented credible efforts to do so. However, the Oriental Beauty frame used a seemingly similar strategy with the opposite effect: promotion of transnational identity politics. In the Dutch and Chinese *Vogue*, the HI was reframed in ways that removed most of its moral and political significance. However, because the HI involved a formal ongoing pledge, the content of the Chinese and Dutch *Vogue* was still permanently altered for 'cosmopolitical' reasons: an attempt to redress what the HI manifesto identifies as a global wrong.

Our analysis of media responses to *Vogue*'s moral initiatives under-scores *Vogue*'s capacity to address transnational audiences. In the USA,

Vogue is both object and initiator of public engagement and debate. In China, *Vogue* is more initiator than object. Its public role is most visible in its promotion of Oriental beauty; but there is little media debate about the role of *Vogue*. In Dutch media, *Vogue* functions mainly as a symbol of the transnational beauty world, which is cast as unhealthy, glamorous and deeply un-Dutch. Both international and Dutch *Vogue* are object, rather than initiator of debate and engagement.

These national variations reflect each country's differential relation to and position in the transnational fashion field. These differences were most evident in responses to the HI. American media cautiously embraced it and went on to behave as a watchdog for a global cause that clearly made sense to them. Dutch and Chinese responses were more noncommittal. In Dutch media, *Vogue* is portrayed as an outside force, which automatically limits its moral relevance. In China, the HI initially lacked relevance because the critiques to which it responds have not been central to public debates. Its relevance quickly increased when Chinese *Vogue* became the centre of a transnational scandal. However, this scandal contrasted (immoral) Chinese practices with a (moral) international community, which can hardly be conducive to cosmopolitan engagement.

Finally, what can *Vogue* teach us about the possibility of cosmopolitics? First, our findings call attention to the role of elite media institutions in the formation of transnational political or normative engagement. Rather than identify new political issues, *Vogue*'s moral interventions gave shape to existing concerns by making them durable and legitimate. *Vogue* Black and the Oriental Beauty campaigns addressed global racial inequalities, latching onto concerns of globally marginalized groups by aestheticizing and 'consecrating' race-specific beauty. Similarly, the pledges in the HI consecrate international critiques of *Vogue* and make all national versions of *Vogue* vulnerable to transnational critique and correction. Thus, a prestigious institution like *Vogue* has the potential to address transnational publics for existing social concerns and to enlarge such publics by adding high status to moral concern. As an entertainment medium, *Vogue* reaches larger audiences than traditional political media, relying on visual materials that easily transcend national boundaries. However, their effectiveness depends on pre-existing public discourses and on the framing of local actors and institutions.

Second, cosmopolitics may emerge in domains that seem far removed from traditional politics. On the transnational level, traditional political institutions are weak or non-existent, so attempts to organize transnational publics may emerge in a field as frivolous and commercialized as global fashion, around issues not traditionally associated with international politics: beauty and the body. We hypothesize that consumption is a likely breeding ground for cosmopolitics: a global resource for community, identity formation and moral concern that might very well promote global engagement (Soper 2007). Consequently, corporate social responsibility may become crucial to the development of cosmopolitics.

Our study also points to the limits of cosmopolitics. First, the global scope of *Vogue* sometimes gives its interventions a rather hegemonic, top-down character. As we saw in the controversy around the Chinese breach of the HI, what looks like global moral engagement from one angle may seem rather imperialistic from another. When a global institution like *Vogue* spreads moral concerns to transnational publics, these may be experienced as meaningful, but also as hegemonic dictates, quite meaningless, or both. All attempts to address and unite transnational publics rely on local actors, who may decide to adopt, but also to reframe or ignore, the invitation.

Second, the cosmopolitics of *Vogue* paradoxically relies on its exclusivity. It is the exclusion of non-beauty that makes the inclusion of curviness and non-whiteness meaningful. If *Vogue* embraced everything, its openness would lose its capacity to consecrate. This is the paradox of omnivorousness: if openness becomes total acceptance, it stops being a taste, as taste is about discerning and classifying (Bourdieu 1984). A similar paradox applies to all cosmopolitanism. In order to be open-minded, cosmopolitics requires clear standards for excluding or rejecting certain things. 'Citizens of the world' are open to all persons, styles and tastes, from all over the world. However, they have to be discerning. Otherwise, their openness would lose not only its meaning but also its humanistic and moral significance.

Notes

1. Sources: http://www.condenast.com/brands/vogue/media-kit/print; http://www.condenastinternational.com/brand
2. Another prominent moral-political theme, notably in American *Vogue*, is sustainability and ecological awareness.
3. Including Hong Kong and Macao but not Taiwan.
4. The whole issue is available at: http://www.vogue.it/en/vogue-black/the-black-issue/2010/02/cover-black-issue
5. Since all persons quoted are Westerners, it could be a translation from a Western source. The article has no byline.
6. http://www.vogue.com.cn/magazine/current-issue/6446-2.html (translations from Chinese and Dutch are by the authors)
7. Interview J. Bunders, December 3, 2012.
8. http://www.vogue.com.cn/magazine/current-issue/news_1442cf60526124fa.html
9. http://usa.chinadaily.com.cn/2011-04/13/content_12319449.htm
10. For example: http://sn.ifeng.com/shishangpindao/shishangzixun/detail_2012_10/04/364447_0.shtml; http://people.ladymax.cn/201210/08-10212.html

References

Beck, Ulrich. 2002. "The Cosmopolitan Society and Its Enemies?" *Theory, Culture & Society* 19 (1–2): 17–44.doi: 10.1177/026327640201900101.

Bourdieu, Pierre. 1984. *Distinction: A Social Critique of the Judgement of Taste.* London: Routledge.

Calhoun, Craig. 2002. "The Class Consciousness of Frequent Travelers: Toward a Critique of Actually Existing Cosmopolitanism." *South Atlantic Quarterly* 101 (4): 869–897.doi: 10.1215/00382876-101-4-869.

Chow, Yiu Fai. 2011. "Moving, Sensing Intersectionality: A Case Study of Miss China Europe." *Signs* 36 (2): 411–436.doi: 10.1086/656023.

Delanty, Gerard. 2009. *The Cosmopolitan Imagination.* Cambridge: Cambridge University Press.

DeSanctis, Marcia. 2012. "Fashion & Features: The Transformers. How Much Can You Really Change about Your Mind and Body? Three Writers Find Out." *Vogue*, April, p. 54.

deVreese, Claes. 2005. "News Framing: Theory and Typology." *Information Design Journal* 13 (1): 48–59.

Dikötter, Frank. 2003. "The Discourse of Race in Modern China". In *Race and Ethnicity*, edited by John Stone and Dennis Tutledge, 125–135. Malden: Blackwell.

Frith, Katherine, Ping Shaw, and Hong Cheng. 2005. "The Construction of Beauty: A Cross-cultural Analysis of Women's Magazine Advertising." *Journal of Communication* 55 (1): 56–70. doi:10.1111/j.1460-2466.2005.tb02658.x.

Godart, Frédéric, and Ashley Mears. 2009. "How Do Cultural Producers Make Creative Decisions?" *Social Forces* 88 (2): 671–692. doi:10.1111/j.1460-2466.2005.tb02658.x.

Johnston, Josée, and Judith Taylor. 2008. "Feminist Consumerism and Fat Activists: A Comparative Study of Grassroots Activism and the Dove Real Beauty Campaign." *Signs* 33 (4): 941–966. doi:10.1086/528849.

Kruspe, Dana. 2012. "So Did Vogue's 'Health Initiative' Actually Change Anything? We Investigate." *Fashionista.com*, June 25.

Levitt, Peggy, and Nyíri, Pál. forthcoming. "Introduction to Special Issue on Books, Bodies, and Bronzes: Comparing Sites of Global Citizenship Creation." *Ethnic and Racial Studies*.

Lindgreen, Adam, and Valerie Swaen. 2010. "Corporate Social Responsibility." *International Journal of Management Reviews* 12 (10): 1–7. doi:10.1111/j.1468-2370.2009.00277.x.

Mau, Dhani. 2012. "Vogue Germany's Health Initiative Editorial Features a Woman Smoking a Cigarette." *Fashionista.com*, May 18.

Mears, Ashley. 2011 *Pricing Beauty: The Making of a Fashion Model.* Berkeley: University of California Press.

Oliva, Roberto, and Norberto Angeletti. 2006. *In Vogue: The Illustrated History of the World's Most Influential Fashion Magazine.* Milan: Rizzoli.

Phelan, Hayley. 2012. "Vogue Will No Longer Work With Unhealthy-Looking or Under-16 Models." *Fashionista.com*, May 3.

Rognlin, Briana. 2012. "Surprise! Vogue's Health Initiative Covers Aren't So Body Positive." *Blisstree*, June 4. http://www.blisstree.com/2012/06/04/beauty-shopping/vogue-health-initiative-june-covers-not-body-positive-583/.

Saito, Hiro. 2011. "An Actor-Network Theory of Cosmopolitanism." *Sociological Theory* 29 (2): 124–149. doi:10.1111/j.1467-9558.2011.01390.x.

Sauers, Jenna. 2012. "Vogue Says no more Underaged Models." *Jezebel*, May 3. http://jezebel.com/5907361/vogue-says-no-more-underaged-models.

Scott, Lesley. 2008. "Win a Copy of Vogue Italy's All-black Issue." *Fashiontribes. com*, July 24. http://fashiontribes.typepad.com/fashion/2008/07/win-a-copy-of-v.html.

Shih, Shu-Mei. 2013. "Comparison as Relation". In *Comparison: Theories, Approaches, Uses*, edited by Rita Felski and Susan Stanford Friedman, 79–98. Baltimore, MD: Johns Hopkins Press.

Soper, Kate. 2007. "Re-thinking the Good Life: The Citizenship Dimension of Consumer Disaffection with Consumerism." *Journal of Consumer Culture* 7 (2): 205–229. doi:10.1177/1469540507077681.

Stewart, Dodai. 2008. "Italian Vogue's All-black Issue: A Guided Tour." *Jezebel*, July 14. http://jezebel.com/5024967/italian-vogues-all-black-issue-a-guided-tour.

Uitermark, Justus. 2012. *Dynamics of Power in Dutch Integration Politics*. Amsterdam: Amsterdam University Press.

vanZoonen, Liesbet. 2005. *Entertaining the Citizen*. Lanham, MD: Rowman & Littlefield.

Watson, Carol. 2008. "Italian Vogue Selling like the New iPhone." *AdAge*, July 18. http://adage.com/article/the-big-tent/italian-vogue-selling-iphone/129759/.

Wintour, Anna. 2012. "Taking a Stand: International Vogue Editors Join Forces to Support the CFDA's Health Initiative." *Vogue*, June.

Yaeger, Lynn. 2012. "View: Bringing Sexy Back: Best Known For Her Bikini Body, Swimwear Model Kate Upton May Just Seduce The High-Fashion World Yet." *Vogue*, July, p. 54.

Shifting tides of world-making in the UNESCO World Heritage Convention: cosmopolitanisms colliding

Christoph Brumann

The success of UNESCO's 1972 World Heritage Convention has made an entry into the World Heritage List a coveted distinction for tourism, nation-building and economic development. This article traces the evolution of the treaty from sharing responsibility for humanity's most prized sites to sharing the World Heritage List as an exercise in global representation. Growing North–South tensions within the World Heritage Committee are currently producing yet another shift, towards sharing the right among treaty states to have their candidate sites listed and wishes fulfilled. While formerly an especially cosmopolitan section of normally often nationally oriented heritage experts was in command, the new turn coincides with the ascendancy of career diplomats, that is people with cosmopolitan aspirations who, conversely, strive to serve national interests. They too are cosmopolitan at times, but typically for broader concerns such as world peace or global equity that transcend the focus of the Convention.

The UNESCO Convention Concerning the Protection of the World Cultural and Natural Heritage adopted in 1972 has enjoyed a spectacular rise in prominence. Ratified by 190 states, it is one of the most successful international treaties. As of 2013, the World Heritage List includes 981 properties – some of which are themselves a series of many separate component sites – located in 160 states. The Convention is clearly the flagship activity of the United Nations Educational, Scientific and Cultural Organization (UNESCO) these days, despite this organization's educational priorities (Singh 2010). For attracting tourists and boosting national and local self-esteem, the World Heritage title can have a dramatic effect.

Books, magazines, television documentaries, websites and apps enable 'virtual visits' from around the world. World Heritage Studies programmes are opening in universities from Dublin to Tsukuba, creating a new academic sub-field. Even war has been waged over World Heritage: the listing of the ancient Khmer temple of Preah Vihear on territory disputed between Thailand and Cambodia in 2008 led to several bloody clashes between the two armies.

Clearly, World Heritage is a key arena for contemporary world-making[1] and the production of 'globality', defined by Robertson (1992, 132; see also introduction) as 'a consciousness of the world as a single place'. It must be seen as an instance of 'reaching out across cultural differences through dialogue, aesthetic enjoyment, and respect; of living together with difference', as Pnina Werbner (2008, 2) describes cosmopolitanism. World Heritage rests on the assumption that the world's most prized natural and cultural sites belong to all of us, entailing a shared responsibility for their care. Because World Heritage properties are so often included in tourist itineraries, it has taken root in the 'everyday', 'ordinary' (Vertovec and Cohen 2002, 5) or 'vernacular' (Werbner 2008, 14) cosmopolitanisms of people worldwide and is no longer reflective of an 'aloof, globetrotting bourgeois image of cosmopolitanism' (Vertovec and Cohen 2002, 21) that one might be tempted to read into it. The focus of the envisioned global sharing of the World Heritage venture, however, has changed over time. The original emphasis on the co-ownership and co-stewardship of sites by 'humanity' rather than just the respective nation state gave way to an emphasis on the World Heritage List as a shared exercise in world representation. Since 2010, a further shift has occurred: what is now shared is the right of nation states to have their candidates listed, even against conservation-related concerns, and their already listed sites kept free from supranational interference. I argue that this shift corresponds to the replacement of key personnel responsible for decision-making, which means that the guiding cosmopolitanisms have changed as well. While formerly a cosmopolitan subset of normally often nationally oriented heritage experts was in command, the new turn coincides with the ascendancy of career diplomats, that is people with cosmopolitan habituses who, conversely, strive to serve national interests. They too are cosmo-politan at times, but typically for broader concerns such as world peace or global equity that transcend the more narrow Convention goals.[2]

From safeguarding to List representation

World Heritage is the intellectual child of a major globalization push in heritage conservation during the 1960s, at a time when war destructions were still fresh in memory and unprecedented environmental damages threatened cultural and natural treasures across the globe. Standard

UNESCO accounts trace the Convention to the safeguarding campaigns that the organization orchestrated in the 1960s, most famously for the Nubian monuments of Abu Simbel, which were transplanted to a location outside the reach of Aswan Dam waters (Hassan 2007), but also for Borobudur, Mohenjo-daro and Venice. Together, these contributed to conceiving a global responsibility for humanity's most treasured sites. Significant too was the international conference in 1964 where cultural conservationists adopted the Venice Charter – the foundational document of modern historical conservation – and created the International Council of Monuments and Sites (ICOMOS), a worldwide membership association. Yet nature conservation organizations contributed too, such as the International Union for Conservation of Nature (IUCN) and the US National Park Service, whose initiatives for a UN-backed register of national parks and a World Heritage Trust later were eventually fused with those of UNESCO and ICOMOS (Stott 2011). The World Heritage Convention was adopted by the General Conference of UNESCO member states in 1972. The World Heritage Committee met for the first time in 1977, and the following year, the first twelve sites were inscribed on the World Heritage List. It has expanded considerably ever since, far exceeding the around 100 sites initially anticipated (for the early history, see Titchen 1995).

The World Heritage Convention was an innovative instrument of international rights, transcending the simple regulation of bilateral interactions between sovereign nation states by postulating a supranational level of concern, the 'common heritage of humanity'. This paralleled developments in the international regulation of the high seas, outer space and Antarctica (Wolfrum 2009). It is also comparable to 'cosmopolitan harm conventions' (CHCs) (Linklater 2002) that have flourished in more recent years, such as the UN human rights conventions, except that it is spaces rather than individuals that are being protected from nation-state willfulness and negligence.

But even though a global heritage commons was formulated, responsibility for it rests with the nation-state signatories who are the operative arms of the Convention. Only they can nominate sites, which must be within their own borders, in the order they see fit. To be inscribed on the list, candidate sites must demonstrate 'outstanding universal value' (OUV) according to one or more of six cultural and four natural criteria.[3] The text files produced to prove this have grown from a handful of pages to huge tomes that take years to prepare. Once nominated, the candidates are then evaluated by ICOMOS (cultural sites) or IUCN (natural sites) through a peer-review style consultation of experts and an on-site inspection. The advisory bodies then either recommend that sites are included in the list, that they be rejected, or that the decision is postponed because minor ('referral') or major ('deferral') revisions are needed.

ICOMOS and IUCN are non-state entities that are globally rather than nationally constituted, but final decisions are made at the annual session of the World Heritage Committee, a body composed of twenty-one nation states elected by all 'States Parties' (i.e. signatory states) in the biannual General Assembly. When this Committee decides to put a site on the list, it acquires the right to monitor (through ICOMOS, IUCN and the World Heritage Center, that is the Convention secretariat within UNESCO headquarters in Paris) how it is conserved and protected. The World Heritage Fund is available to support nominations and conservation measures. Yet officially, inscription presupposes the nominating state's capacity to care for the site with its own resources; only the poorest states can hope for financial aid from this limited fund.[4] The secretariat and advisory bodies often complain that their strained budgets make meeting even core obligations a challenge, a stark contrast to the global visibility of the World Heritage brand and the significant resources that nation states spend to promote their candidacies. A true co-ownership that would transfer authority to a transnational agency with enforcement capabilities and an independent conservation budget has never been considered.

Yet if a global sharing of *sites* has remained elusive, the global sharing of the World Heritage *List* as an exercise in representing the world appeared more within reach. It was only in the last moment that the idea of a celebratory list – and not just a simple register of sites in need of urgent international support – was included in the Convention text (cf. Titchen 1995, 147–151). The first inscriptions contained quite a number of African candidates[5] and until 1990, India – not Italy or Spain as would happen later – was the overall leader in the number of World Heritage properties.[6] An awareness of the benefits of the title combined with the ability to muster sufficient resources to prepare the nomination, however, soon led to a preponderance of (most often Western) European listings and an implicit conceptualization of World Heritage around the typical built heritage of this world region – Italy alone had ten sites inscribed in a single year (1997).[7] Also, while initially a balance between natural and cultural sites was envisaged, cultural nominations clearly predominate. As early as the 1980s, doubts arose about whether a list with over half of its sites located on a single continent could paint a faithful picture of humanity's cultural and natural wonders.

One countermeasure would have been to dampen the nominating fervour of the List leaders. But because these are often among the Committee members, many of which use their term of office (previously six and now four years) to promote their own candidate sites, nomination quotas or moratoriums have received only lukewarm support, often watered down on the next possible occasion. Even the crisis brought about by the USA's suspension of UNESCO dues after the acceptance of Palestine as a full member in 2011 – leading to a budget cut of 22% – could not slow down the nomination stream: the budget working group submitted to pressure from those Committee states that have their internal nomination schedules filled for years in advance.

As a result, European states were never blocked from nominating their European-style heritage sites. The personnel that ICOMOS and IUCN entrusted with reviews and missions and who attended Committee sessions were overwhelmingly from Western European and North American states too. They usually justified this by the difficulty of finding qualified personnel from other regions with the necessary English and French language skills and only seriously started to recruit more broadly in the 2000s. What seemed normal and natural to heritage experts from a very limited part of the world thus influenced how World Heritage took shape. Yet, compared to their professional colleagues who by their training, language skills, interests and the exigencies of conservation legislation are often very much bound to a national frame of reference, the particular selection of experts becoming involved in World Heritage matters are on the cosmopolitan side, and the reform measures tackling the much-deplored Eurocentrism of World Heritage also originated with them.

Redefining cultural heritage

These reform measures, adopted mainly during the 1990s, redefined cultural heritage in more inclusive and less Eurocentric ways, by expanding its scope rather than by restricting or redefining any of its established categories. The Global Strategy for a Representative, Balanced and Credible World Heritage List,[8] adopted by the Committee in 1994, recommended a turn away from palaces, cathedrals and town centres, to include the vestiges of ordinary people and everyday life in their full diversity. This has 'anthropologized' the inscriptions very much: peasant villages, technical and industrial heritage, icons of modern architecture and urban planning, prehistoric sites, and connections of all kinds such as trade and pilgrimage routes, canals and railway lines are now much more common among new inscriptions. Examples of what has alternatively been called 'negative', 'difficult', 'dark' or 'dissonant' heritage (Tunbridge and Ashworth 1996; Logan and Reeves 2008) have increased over recent years, including sites connected to the slave trade and other forms of forced migration, or with deliberate heritage destruction, such as Mostar or Bamiyan. The category of cultural landscapes (Mitchell et al. 2009), introduced in 1992 largely as the brainchild of the World Heritage Center and ICOMOS (Gfeller 2013), accounts for a large number of the nominations now. Celebrating the interaction of humans with their environment, it includes designed landscapes such as parks, cultivated landscapes such as rice terraces, and 'associative landscapes' of mythical or spiritual significance, of which there may be hardly any physical traces (see also Brumann 2013).

The World Heritage Committee has also grown particularly fond of sites that themselves express cosmopolitanism and the meeting of societies and cultures. Transborder nominations composed of a series of spatially separate components within two or more countries are exempted from the usual nomination quotas (currently one property and one cultural landscape per state and year). In the case of the forced migration sites mentioned above too, human movement is transnational or even transcontinental. Further cases include the Bahá'i Holy Places in Haifa and the Western Galilee (inscribed in 2008) – centre of a global pilgrimage tradition – or the Osun-Osogbo Sacred Grove in Osogbo, Nigeria (2005; see Probst 2011). Two gigantic transborder nominations for the Central and East Asian Silk Road sites[9] and for the Qhapaq Ñan,[10] the road system of the Inca Empire, await inscription in 2014.

Notions of authenticity too have been expanded and made more cosmopolitan. From the beginning, all World Heritage properties were to meet a test of authenticity, understood in the spirit of Venice Charter conservational orthodoxy, which tolerates reconstruction only in exceptional circumstances and if clearly distinguished from the original fabric. Yet, Japan's 1993 nomination of the Hôryûji near Nara, a temple complex containing the oldest wooden buildings on earth from the seventh and eighth century, kicked off a fundamental debate, given that in time-honoured Japanese fashion, these structures have been repeatedly dismantled and reassembled over the centuries, with substantial replacement of damaged material. While some European experts advocated a strict line, they eventually lost out, and instead, an expert meeting in 1994 drafted the Nara Document on Authenticity,[11] which authorized a whole array of additional criteria in which authenticity can manifest itself – not just material, form or design, but also fairly elusive ones such as 'traditions, techniques and management systems; location and setting; language, and other forms of intangible heritage; spirit and feeling'.[12] In essence, the Committee recognized the cultural relativism of authenticity standards since 'cultural heritage must be considered and judged primarily within the cultural contexts to which it belongs' (§81). These reforms, too, opened doors for new candidates (see also Brumann 2013).

There is therefore no doubt that the World Heritage List is less dominated by conventional European perspectives now and operates according to a more inclusive definition of heritage. This is, to a large extent, the result of the work of the more cosmopolitan-minded members of a predominantly Euro-American class of heritage experts. A Japanese participant in the Nara conference, for example, recalled how Euro-American participants brought high hopes for finding a fundamentally different conservation philosophy in Japan, almost as if seeking redemption from the confines of Western conceptions. Correspondingly, the main drafters of the Nara Document were Euro-American, not Japanese. The introduction of the cultural landscape category, too, involved major input from Euro-Americans (see also Gfeller 2013), even when the category was devised with sites from the Global South in mind. Clearly, these conservationists were trying hard to transcend their traditional categories and arrive at something more truly global, and they did so from a largely idealistic concern to keep the World Heritage endeavour intellectually convincing.

During the 2000s, rather than instituting further programmatic innovations, the Committee systematized World Heritage, with procedures for nomination, inscription, monitoring, decision-making and documentation standardized and often substantially elaborated. It is tempting to see this as evidence of the spread of 'governmentality' (Foucault 2003) where only what is known, documented – statistically if possible – and procedurally specified can be governed, and ultimately expected to govern itself, in an economically viable way. Yet, while central value indicators for natural sites, such as biodiversity or the presence of endemic species, can indeed be quantified, a truly operational definition of OUV for the cultural sites has yet to be arrived at. What have been pursued instead are verbal rather than statistical definitions of OUV for individual World Heritage properties in the so-called Statements of Outstanding Universal Value, which have been increasingly emphasized in recent years. Moreover, new nominations must now include a comparative analysis that assesses the site within the context of other national and international sites both on and not on the World Heritage List.

There are clear limits to governmentality here: far from all the statements of OUV define the heritage value and baseline condition of conservation in a measurable way, and quite a few comparative analyses simply line up descriptions of individual sites without a clear conclusion. In session debates, reference to precedent cases is also less frequent than might be expected, with delegates missing even the obvious parallels. Notwithstanding, these exercises do contribute to the creation of a shared space of reference that the World Heritage properties inhabit, unique as each one of them is required to be, and this is certainly on the minds, if not of stressed session participants, then of the teachers and students of the specialized university programmes. Much more than before, World Heritage has become a 'global system of common difference' in Richard Wilk's (1995) sense. Creating a system that renders all individual sites comparable and commensurable, bringing them on a fundamentally equal plane, is certainly a cosmopolitan move.

Cosmopolitan too is the effect of the stream of international expert meetings that the Committee summons on specific heritage categories and Convention issues around the globe and throughout the year; the periodic reporting exercise that brings together national heritage institutions and local site managers of World Heritage properties in preparatory meetings; the training programmes offered by the third advisory body of the Convention, the International Centre for the Study of the Preservation and Restoration of Cultural Property (ICCROM) in Rome; and the growing number of Category 2 Centers (approved by UNESCO but funded by specific nation states) that specialize in research and training on certain types and/or regions of World Heritage. These activities greatly contribute to the distribution of shared standards of site conservation, management and presentation, and the formation of a global class of heritage experts.

In sum, while not leading to a true co-ownership of World Heritage sites, the developments of the 1990s and 2000s contributed to a more inclusive conception of the World Heritage List and the formation of a set of institutions and experts strongly committed to this cosmopolitan vision. This is all the more remarkable because modern conservation took shape during, and owes a lot to, nineteenth-century high nationalism (Larkham 1996). The fact that conservation regulations must be in conversation with property rights, urban planning strategies and taxation inevitably binds much heritage administration to a national, if not provincial or municipal, frame of reference. The background disciplines of heritage conservationists too, such as art history, architectural history or archaeology, often have distinct national specificities and thematic focuses, at least in Europe, and have, in the past, provided the scaffolding for the idea of civilizational greatness where the superiority of European and other 'high cultures' is very much taken for granted. Early international exchanges and borrowings in the field of heritage conservation did occur but were largely confined to Europe and North America or were the product of colonial imposition (Hall 2011; Swenson 2013; Swenson and Mandler 2013).

This means that conservationists are not 'natural' cosmopolitans – different from, say, anthropologists for whom the symbolism of a mud hut can be as grandiose as a baroque palace. The cosmopolitan striving of the Euro-American conservationists involved in World Heritage conceptual reform has to be appreciated accordingly, not as something that comes with the trade but as a genuine effort to transcend boundaries and inbuilt biases that would not concern most of their national colleagues. We detect here the 'willingness to engage with the Other' and the 'intellectual and aesthetic stance of openness toward divergent cultural experiences' that Hannerz (1990, 239) identifies as the marks of the true cosmopolitan.

From a representative List to equal List access

These efforts have not produced the desired results, however. The push for systematization has made the application process more demanding: the nomination manual (UNESCO 2011) itself has 140 pages. The advisory bodies are more likely to pick up on inconsistencies in the nomination files, such as deficiencies in the comparative analysis or the protection and management framework. States with developed nomination appetites and resources are more able to cope with such demands and have adapted to the new conceptual wave. Italy (six sites as of 2013) and France (five sites)[13] lead the cultural landscape category, which, although invented for rice terraces or sacred mountains, includes a host of European wine regions now.

Countries from the Global South, by contrast, often struggle with the more stringent requirements, yet their governments are impatient to see tangible benefits flow from the World Heritage title. When the strict conservation line gets in the way of resource extraction or tourism development, it is then seen as a luxury that the rich states of the North can more easily afford and to which they should actively contribute. More than once, informants from the South invoked the Abu Simbel campaign as the true model to which the World Heritage Convention should aspire.

Mounting dissatisfaction finally erupted into the open in the 2010 Committee session in Brasilia. Starting with the debate over whether the Galapagos Islands should be removed from the List of World Heritage in Danger – IUCN acknowledged that remedial measures had been taken but they still fell short – Committee state representatives supported each other and the non-Committee states in each having their own national wishes fulfilled. The Galapagos Islands were removed from the Danger List according to Ecuador's wishes, decisions on other problematic sites were softened, and the number of new inscriptions doubled from those that the advisory bodies had endorsed. Mutual support among Committee states is not at all costly – there are quotas for nominations but theoretically, all submitted candidates could make it onto the List since OUV is believed to be an absolute quality. Instead, helping one another out among states encourages return favours in due course. Also, with close to 1,000 sites on the list, the marginal cost of additional inscriptions to the exclusiveness of the title has become tiny, and in spite of some press criticism of the recent turn (The Economist 2010; Stührenberg 2011), there have been no perceptible dents in the public traction of the World Heritage title. The new mores have persisted through the subsequent Committee meetings in Paris (2011), Saint Petersburg (2012) and Phnom Penh (2013) (see also Meskell 2012, 2013). If anything, resistance to the free-for-all has weakened: while for quite a few decisions in Brasilia, secret ballots were called – a more or less open invitation to other state representatives to breach their negotiated promises – this hardly occurred in subsequent sessions. Increasingly also, ICOMOS and IUCN are overruled almost without debate, lessening the need for the (often rather improvized) arguments still presented in 2010.

These changes were possible because of the composition of the 2010 Committee. North America was not represented at all and Western Europe was mainly represented by less powerful states such as Sweden, Switzerland and Estonia. These three delegations supported the advisory bodies' recommendations and the independence of the Committee from nation-state interests. But they could more easily afford to do so since they had realized national World Heritage aspirations in the past: in terms of sites per population, they outperformed all other eighteen Committee members at that point. Many of the defenders of national interests, by contrast, were regional political heavyweights and/or BRIC and G20 members, such as Mexico, Brazil, Nigeria, Egypt, South Africa, Russia and China. France and Australia were also present but because they had their own nominations up for decision, they had to tread lightly for fear of reprisals from other colleagues. (State delegates readily acknowledge this special conflict of interests.) Australia, in particular, no longer acted as the champion of proper practice that it had been the previous year. Interestingly, all inscriptions made against the advisory bodies' recommendations in Brasilia were for sites outside Europe and North America, making for the least Eurocentric distribution of new listings in decades.[14]

Yet, while there was a clear North–South dimension to this initial breach of the fortress, in the following meetings the tendency has been to abide by all national wishes, South or North, and newly elected members such as India, Japan and Germany – which invariably arrive with their own candidate sites – have gone with the flow, rather than joining the resisters. Also, simply ignoring the advisory bodies has given way to attempts to actively re-educate them, such as by urging them to cultivate a 'dialogue' with the states (a euphemism for attention to their wishes).

Much of this arises as the simple consequence of nation-state delegates pursuing their national interests with whatever means at hand, either openly or through quid pro quo arrangements with their peers. This inclination had been present for a long time but had been tempered by a general reluctance to overrule the advisory bodies and their advice. Yet, the sessions since 2010 have clearly established a new culture where ignoring the 'spoilsports' has become commonplace, something that is denounced by some treaty states not currently on the Committee and also criticized by a recent external audit of the Global Strategy (WHC-11/18. GA/8), but nothing about which Committee delegates intent on fulfilling their orders must be too concerned. Increasingly, there is a sense that World Heritage inscription is an entitlement that should be generously shared rather than jealously guarded in the name of abstract considerations such as consistency. This means that the focus is shifting, from the List and its capacity to adequately represent and protect the world's cultural and natural jewels to the nation states' equal right to slots on the List.

The ascendancy of career diplomats

Orchestrating Committee support for national interests is the task of the diplomats dispatched to UNESCO headquarters where most member states are represented by a 'permanent delegate' of ambassador rank. While these delegates are often sent from ministries of education, science or culture in the case of the Southern states, the Northern states prefer ordinary diplomats (see also Singh 2010, 31). They are generalists with backgrounds in fields such as law, economics or international relations who will be transferred elsewhere or back home after a few years. Those ambassadors who are not career diplomats often have a foreign-ministry staffer as deputy.

The ascendancy of career diplomats in the World Heritage arena has occurred mainly since the 2000s. Old-timers among the delegation experts still remember Committee sessions that they went to without foreign service support, meaning that the (largely Euro-American) heritage experts were among professional peers. Yet nowadays, almost all Committee state delegations are headed by the permanent delegate to UNESCO or someone even higher up in the foreign ministry, and these diplomats also speak for the delegation most of the time. This reflects the growing importance of World Heritage to national governments, themselves under pressure by provinces and municipalities that want sites under their jurisdiction listed, protected from Committee interference, and so on. Obviously, states now agree that something as important as World Heritage cannot be left to political amateurs.

Career diplomats are cosmopolitans by profession, conversant in several languages, world politics and the refined lifestyles of capitals around the globe (for a close-up ethnography, see Neumann 2012). Those dispatched to UNESCO meet frequently on a range of topics in the headquarter buildings where many have their offices. They develop first-name friendships with wide-armed hugs and cheek-kissing when meeting each other in the corridors or at the frequent social events. They exude a clear sense that it is them, not the headquarter bureaucrats or technical experts, who are in command at UNESCO. In fact, most governing boards in UNESCO are filled with such state representatives who then decide what the international civil servants in the organization's service must implement. While the heritage experts attending the World Heritage sessions may know each other for a longer time, the diplomats interact more frequently and intensely and, on average, outperform the experts in terms of self-confidence, social grace, linguistic skills and eloquence.

Yet, the diplomats are also more unequivocally committed to their country's interests, and their personal careers depend on their success in achieving favourable solutions and negotiating the hidden deals of mutual support that then smooth the way for their national plans. To a considerable degree, they are habitual cosmopolitans who use this capacity for non-cosmopolitan ends – a configuration that, as outlined above, is exactly the reverse of the heritage experts attracted to the World Heritage sessions. For Hannerz (1990, 239), the diplomats would not qualify for 'true cosmopolitanism', and they would rather fit into the 'cosmocrat' category of globally mobile but eventually self-centred rather than world-centred elites proposed by Micklethwait and Wooldridge (2003, 221–242).

Yet, the diplomats too have their cosmopolitan ideals for those matters where they are not under orders. These concern aspects other than heritage conservation, however, such as global equity and the peaceful interaction between nation states. One Western European diplomat, for example, voiced his misgivings to me when in the session, an ICOMOS representative had pointed to historical destructions in one candidate site to question its OUV. The diplomat was appalled how there was no awareness that colonial troops from that representative's own country had been the destroyers. Also, he could find nothing wrong with 'the others' (i.e. non-European states) getting their share of the World Heritage pie too.

A considerable amount of diplomatic attention also goes to the ostensibly peaceful settlements of issues around politically sensitive properties. Because discussing them openly in the sessions would lead to hours of typecast statements and hostilities, it is common practice to hold separate negotiations alongside the sessions – the so-called 'side tables'. Only the concerned parties and agreed mediators are present, with the latter sometimes shuttling between different rooms. Such special treatment has been extended to the Israeli sites on disputed ground such as the Old City of Jerusalem – nominated by Jordan and inscribed before Israel ratified the Convention – for a long time. More recent cases include Preah Vihear, the medieval monasteries in Kosovo (claimed by Serbia) and the Church of the Nativity in Bethlehem (inscribed by Palestine). If such negotiations achieve their goal, the Committee is presented with a draft decision text, which the chairperson then proposes to adopt without debate.

The interesting point is that participating diplomats tend to see this as a success. In the 2012 session in Saint Petersburg, the negotiated postpone-ment of the debate over putting the Bagrati Cathedral in Georgia on the Danger List was greeted by diplomats with relief, given the challenge that discussing a major symbol of Georgian nationalism on the territory of, and presided over by, the arch-enemy would have presented. This meant, however, that the controversial reconstruction project backed by President Saakashvili could be completed without further Committee interference. In another example, in the run-up to the 2013 session, a Western diplomat told me how pleased all his colleagues were about recent Israeli–Palestinian negotiations about the Old City of Jerusalem, not because of conservation but rather because there was, at long last, one topic over which the two adversaries were really sitting at the same table. Clearly, the individual sites take a back seat to the diplomatic cosmopolitan vision, that of ostensible harmony within the family of nations.

The rule of diplomats whose commitments are either more national or broader than simply conserving World Heritage may be coming to an end, however. Pressure is mounting, and advance deal-making is taking place not just between UNESCO ambassador peers but also between foreign ministries and heads of government. Transfer or demotion are real possibilities if the expectations are not met. Here, the Committee decision taken on the last session day in 2011, in an exhausted and clearly inattentive hall, to live stream future sessions on the internet may become momentous. Critics of the current developments hoped for a restraining effect on horse-trading. In the 2012 session, however, informants reported that several delegations were 'on remote control' with their home ministries who were watching the broadcast and texting them detailed instructions about how to proceed. One delegate was even rumoured to have been called home right away when he did not say precisely what his national president had promised to a colleague in office. In other interventions too, the delegates' sense of being watched by their national and site constituencies was obvious. This means that the World Heritage Committee sessions, while more globally accessible than ever, encourage parochial and self-serving behaviour. If cosmopolitanism is involved at all here, it is only in the sense of according equal rights to politically and economically manifestly unequal nation states, in this case the equal right to have their favourites listed and protected from supranational interference.

Conclusion

The World Heritage Convention, now in its fifth decade, has emerged as a crucial tool for world-making and for driving forward a cosmopolitan imagination. Yet, the cosmopolitanism that has guided this trajectory has moved through several successive stages. To adequately characterize these, it is useful to distinguish between cosmopolitan habituses and cosmopolitan aspirations, and to highlight that the two do not always occur together. The Convention was initially put in place to create globally protected enclaves within national territories. Because the UN framework remains inter- rather than transnational, this was never fully implemented, as the Convention states functioned as the executive arm of the Convention. Instead, a small class of heritage experts with cosmopolitan ambitions set about to define World Heritage in a more universalist and inclusive way, thereby transcending their own often rather nationally defined training and orientation.

Yet, with attention growing and key practices of the World Heritage system – such as the nomination machinery of the nation states – simply rolling on, the tide has shifted since around the late 1990s. Now, it is people with cosmopolitan habituses but thoroughly national assignments that dominate the arena – the career diplomats dispatched by nation states to UNESCO in Paris. They excel in the art of deal-making for fulfilling the orders of the ministerial superiors, and much of what happens at the sessions is simply the result of their strategic pursuit of these priorities with all available means.

That these agendas are determined by national interests is, in my view, a consequence of the enormous success of World Heritage. Precisely by having become a global canon and gold standard of value, it provokes national and local ambitions to secure a place on the world map, as a participant from a remote island state phrased it to me after their candidate site was included in the List. As in other global competitions such as the Olympic Games, people can be both good global citizens who embrace cosmopolitan ideals and obsessed with the national medal count at the same time. In my observations of the World Heritage Commission sessions, it struck me just how normal and expected the pursuit of national interests is, even among experts and participants who are paragons of universalist ideals as long as their own national sites are not on the agenda. That the tide would turn nation-centred at some point is therefore no surprise, particularly when a profession like diplomacy, whose major task is to represent national interests, is in the driving seat.

Still, diplomats too have cosmopolitan aspirations. But their actual cosmopolitan projects sidestep the relatively humdrum concerns of individual site protection and heritage conservation and focus instead on achieving peaceful intercourse among a family of nations increasingly seen as one of equals. And since, unlike the zero-sum Olympic Games, the gold medals at the World Heritage Committee sessions (read: inscriptions on the List) can simply be multiplied, there are no obstacles to generously sharing inscriptions and making one's peers happy, even when this comes at the expense of site conservation; the workloads of the advisory bodies and the secretariat, which have to take care of an ever-growing number of properties; and the overall consistency of the List. In fact, the World Heritage Committee may be entering a post-cosmopolitan phase, if the latest trend of controlling delegates from afar by watching their deliberations online takes root. Just as computerized stock trade may sideline or at least decentralize the community of brokers, so Committee sessions conducted in this way would no longer require the presence of cosmopolitans, but rather mere mouthpieces of bilateral national strategizing.

This case illustrates that there are different ways to be cosmopolitan and global citizens and that we would do well to distinguish between them. We should not be surprised when cosmopolitan ambitions go hand in hand with national ones. The heritage experts in this account moved from national traditions to a cosmopolitan vision, while the career diplomats, who are cosmopolitan professionals sent in to achieve national goals, follow the reverse trajectory.

Acknowledgements

I thank the two anonymous reviewers, the special issue editors, and Aurélie Elisa Gfeller for their helpful comments.

Funding

This study was funded by a Heisenberg Fellowship of the German Research Association (DFG) and the Department 'Resilience and Transformation in Eurasia' of the Max Planck Institute for Social Anthropology, Halle (Germany).

Notes

1.   I owe this phrase to Richard Rottenburg who after one of my presentations on the topic exclaimed 'Hier wird Welt gemacht!' (Here, world is being made).
2.   My analysis rests on an ethnographic approach, combining participant observation of all World Heritage Committee and General Assembly sessions in 2009–12 and other statutory meetings and conferences, interviews with key individuals from many participating organizations, and a study of the extensive documentary record. For details of the research setting and methodology, see Brumann (2012).
3.   http://whc.unesco.org/en/criteria
4.   Expenditures in the 2010–11 biennium were at US$6.8 million (document WHC-12/36.COM/15.Rev, 2).
5.   cf. http://whc.unesco.org/en/list/stat
6.   cf. http://whc.unesco.org/en/list
7.   cf. http://whc.unesco.org/en/statesparties/it
8.   http://whc.unesco.org/en/globalstrategy
9.   http://whc.unesco.org/en/news/870
10.   http://whc.unesco.org/en/qhapaqnan
11.   http://www.international.icomos.org/naradoc_eng.htm
12.   Operational Guidelines for the Implementation of the World Heritage Convention, §82; http://whc.unesco.org/en/guidelines
13.   cf. http://whc.unesco.org/en/culturallandscape
14.   cf. http://whc.unesco.org/en/list/stat

References

Brumann, Christoph. 2012. "Multilateral Ethnography: Entering the World Heritage Arena." *Max Planck Institute for Social Anthropology Working Paper 136.* http://www.eth.mpg.de/cms/en/publications/working_papers/pdf/mpi-eth-working-paper-0136.pdf.

Brumann, Christoph. 2013. "Comment le patrimoine mondial de l'Unesco devient immatériel [How UNESCO World Heritage is Becoming Intangible]." *Gradhiva* 18: 23–49.

Foucault, Michel. 2003. "Governmentality." In *The Essential Foucault*, edited by Paul Rabinow and Nikolas Rose, 229–245. New York: The New Press.

Gfeller, Aurélie Elisa. 2013. "Negotiating the Meaning of Global Heritage: 'Cultural Landscapes' in the UNESCO World Heritage Convention, 1972–92." *Journal of Global History* 8 (3): 483–503. doi:10.1017/S1740022813000387.

Hall, Melanie, ed. 2011. *Towards World Heritage: International Origins of the Preservation Movement 1870–1930.* Farnham: Ashgate.

Hannerz, Ulf. 1990. "Cosmopolitans and Locals in World Culture." In *Global Culture: Nationalism, Globalization and Modernity*, edited by Mike Featherstone, 237–252. London: Sage.

Hassan, Fekri. 2007. "The Aswan High Dam and the International Rescue Nubia Campaign." *African Archaeological Review* 24 (3): 73–94. doi:10.1007/s10437-007-9018-5.

Larkham, Peter J. 1996. *Conservation and the City*. London: Routledge. doi:10.4324/9780203320556.

Linklater, Andrew. 2002. "Cosmopolitan Harm Conventions." In *Conceiving Cosmopolitanism: Theory, Context and Practice*, edited by Steven Vertovec and Robin Cohen, 254–267. Oxford: Oxford University Press.

Logan, William Stewart, and Keir Reeves, eds. 2008. *Places of Pain and Shame: Dealing with 'Difficult Heritage'*. London: Routledge.

Meskell, Lynn. 2012. "The Rush to Inscribe: Reflections on the 35th Session of the World Heritage Committee, UNESCO Paris, 2011." *Journal of Field Archaeology* 37 (2): 145–151. doi:10.1179/0093469012Z.00000000014.

Meskell, Lynn. 2013. "UNESCO's World Heritage Convention at 40: Challenging the Economic and Political Order of International Heritage Conservation." *Current Anthropology* 54 (4): 483–494. doi:10.1086/671136.

Micklethwait, John, and Adrian Wooldridge. 2003. *A Future Perfect: The Challenge and Promise of Globalization*. New York: Random House Trade Paperbacks.

Mitchell, Nora, Mechtild Rössler, and Pierre-Marie Tricaud, eds. 2009. *World Heritage Cultural Landscapes: A Handbook for Conservation and Management*. Paris: UNESCO.

Neumann, Iver B. 2012. *At Home with the Diplomats: Inside a European Foreign Ministry*. Ithaca: Cornell University Press.

Probst, Peter. 2011. *Osogbo and the Art of Heritage: Monuments, Deities, and Money*. Bloomington: Indiana University Press.

Robertson, Roland. 1992. *Globalization: Social Theory and Global Culture*. London: Sage.

Singh, J. P. 2010. *United Nations Educational, Scientific, and Cultural Organization (UNESCO): Creating Norms for a Complex World*. London: Routledge.

Stott, Peter H. 2011. "The World Heritage Convention and the National Park Service, 1962–1972." *The George Wright Forum* 28 (3): 279–290.

Stührenberg, Michael. 2011. "Von Trümmern und Träumen [Of Debris and Dreams]." *Geo* 55: 52–70.

Swenson, Astrid. 2013. *The Rise of Heritage: Preserving the Past in France, Germany and England, 1789–1914*. Cambridge: Cambridge University Press.

Swenson, Astrid, and Peter Mandler, eds. 2013. *From Plunder to Preservation: Britain and the Heritage of Empire, c.1800–1940*. Oxford: Oxford University Press. doi:10.5871/bacad/9780197265413.001.0001.

The Economist. 2010. "A Danger List in Danger." *The Economist*, August 26. http://www.economist.com/node/16891951.

Titchen, Sarah M. 1995. "On the Construction of Outstanding Universal Value: UNESCO's World Heritage Convention (Convention Concerning the Protection of the World Cultural and Natural Heritage, 1972) and the Identification and Assessment of Cultural Places for Inclusion in the World Heritage List." Unpublished PhD diss., Australian National University.

Tunbridge, J. E., and G. J. Ashworth. 1996. *Dissonant Heritage: The Management of the Past as a Resource in Conflict.* Chichester: J. Wiley.

UNESCO. 2011. *Preparing World Heritage Nominations.* http://whc.unesco.org/uploads/activities/documents/activity-643-1.pdf.

Vertovec, Steven, and Robin Cohen. 2002. "Introduction: Conceiving Cosmopolitanism." In *Conceiving Cosmopolitanism: Theory, Context and Practice,* edited by Steven Vertovec and Robin Cohen, 1–22. Oxford: Oxford University Press.

Werbner, Pnina. 2008. "Introduction: Towards a New Cosmopolitan Anthropology." In *Anthropology and the New Cosmopolitanism: Rooted, Feminist and Vernacular Perspectives,* edited by Pnina Werbner, 1–29. New York: Berg.

Wilk, Richard R. 1995. "Learning to be Local in Belize: Global Systems of Common Difference." In *Worlds Apart: Modernity through the Prism of the Local,* edited by Daniel Miller, 110–133. London: Routledge.

Wolfrum, Rüdiger. 2009. "Common Heritage of Mankind." In *Max Planck Encyclopedia of Public International Law,* edited by Rüdiger Wolfrum. http://www.mpepil.com.

Cosmopolitan theology: Fethullah Gülen and the making of a 'Golden Generation'

Thijl Sunier

Global conditions, under which an increasing number of Muslims in the world currently live, do not just generate idioms of purity often adduced to global Islam, but also new and diverse forms of sociability and notions of global citizenship. This article addresses, as an example in case, *Hizmet*, one of the fastest growing contemporary Islamic movements. *Hizmet* and its founder Fethullah Gülen propagate a global Islamic doctrine with explicitly cosmopolitan underpinnings. However, there seems to be a contradiction between the cosmopolitan inclusiveness and universality of Gülen's global message, and strong internal hierarchical structures and the disciplining modes of teaching and training that are applied by the movement to teach the doctrine. I will argue that there is no contradiction between these two aspects when we focus on the central position of 'hermeneutics of the self' and civic responsibility in Gülen's theology.

Introduction

Ever since the global dimensions of Islam have become an important focus of scholarly interest in the early 2000s, there has been a debate on how contemporary global conditions transform modes of religious reasoning and the particular ways in which religious communities are reconstituted and readdressed (Eickelman and Anderson 2003). There are two more or less opposing positions in this debate. One is that globalization, migration and the increasing encounter of people of different backgrounds have engendered discourses of purity and exclusiveness among Muslims. Thus Roy (2002) argues that globalization has caused a reshaping of the relationship between Muslims and Islam in a world where Muslims have to confront Westernization and live in societies where they constitute a minority. This has contributed to the emergence of a utopian world view of

Islamic purity based on the earliest Islamic sources as the only effective defence against encounters with the 'other'. It is a world view that 'deculturalizes' and 'dehistoricizes', in short 'objectifies', Islam as a universal ideology (Roy 2002, 22). Kepel (2000) takes a similar view, arguing that globalization has resulted in an exploration of how the principle of *ummah* gets transformed into a global frame of ideological reference. According to Appiah (2006), global Islam or 'global fundamentalism' as he calls it, is a religious normative frame of reference that explicitly refutes the inevitable and fundamental process of hybridization and 'cultural contamination' generated by increased global exchange and interaction. Global fundamentalism rejects the necessity to develop competences not only to live *in* a world of strangers but to live *with* strangers. Thus, according to Appiah, global fundamentalism is 'counter-cosmopolitanism'.[1]

The other position holds that the global conditions under which an increasing number of Muslims in the world currently live do not just generate idioms of purity; rather, they create new and diverse forms of sociability that constitute new Muslim self-understandings and religious practices and an increasing diversification of Muslim world views (Leichtman and Schulz 2012). There are numerous examples of modern religious leaders who act on a global scale, explicitly speak to the global political arena, and use Islam to propose models for civility, responsibility and civic engagement. They address the issue of global citizenship by pointing to new forms of responsibility that global encounters necessitate (see e.g. Bowen 1993, 2010; De Koning 2008; Hefner and Zaman 2007, 2, 242; Hoesterey 2012). In many cases, the production of religious authority and knowledge is thoroughly articulated using local, transnational and globally appropriated elements (see e.g. Boender 2007; Zaman 2009; Gräf and Skovgaard 2009).

The *Hizmet* movement

In this article I will discuss an intriguing example of this cosmopolitanization of Islam: the *Hizmet* (service), better known as the 'Gülen movement'. *Hizmet*, founded in Turkey in the 1960s, is one of the fastest growing Islamic movements in the world. They have founded schools, institutions and business companies in more than 100 countries (Van Bruinessen 2010). Founded by its current spiritual leader Fethullah Gülen in the 1960s, it emerged in the early 1980s in response to the changing political and economic environment in Turkey as an important political actor and religious innovative force. In the 1990s, the movement expanded internationally. Today, it is considered one of the most influential Islamic movements in the Turkish political landscape and beyond.

From an originally Turkish nationalist Islamic actor, Fethullah Gülen developed into a genuinely global phenomenon (Agai 2007). Followers often refer to his Islamic doctrine as 'civil Islam', denoting an ethical code for conduct that goes beyond the strictly theological understanding of Islamic ethics. The aim of the educational centres that the movement founded all over the world is to breed a new generation of young Muslims that is capable of acting in today's complex world in a responsible and reflexive way (Yilmaz 2005, 394), which trainees are helped to achieve through a series of introspective exercises. Taking into account the necessary precautions that the editors of this special issue bring up when applying the term cosmopolitanism, the *Hizmet* and the teachings of its founder propagate a global Islamic doctrine with explicitly cosmopolitan underpinnings.

When we focus exclusively on Gülen's teachings, there is much evidence to substantiate this claim. It is produced predominantly by followers who write about Gülen's views on the contemporary global conditions under which Muslims live (see e.g. Carroll 2007; Yilmaz 2007; Çelik 2010; Esposito and Yilmaz 2010). Most of this literature addresses different aspects of Gülen's vision, the origins of his message and why it inspires people. The movement is often presented as a loose network of followers who, in different settings and situations, work and act in the spirit of Gülen. Critics, however, point at the strong internal hierarchical structures and the disciplining modes of teaching and training within the movement.

I argue that there is no contradiction between these two aspects. The assumed inconsistency between a cosmopolitan attitude and mental and bodily discipline is rooted in the so-called individualization thesis of religion. It is predicated on the assumption that religion in modern society is eventually an act of individual self-making, free of disciplinary constraints. However, recent studies on religious subjectivation have pointed at the crucial connection between truth seeking and disciplining practices. They build on what Foucault (1993, 204) has called 'hermeneutics of the self' or 'techniques oriented toward the discovery and the formulation of the truth concerning oneself'. Thus, Asad (1993, 97), in his study on medieval Christian rituals, shows how bodily pain and truth seeking are inextricably linked to one another. In her study on female Muslims in Cairo, Mahmood (2005) points at the seemingly paradoxical relation between subordination and agency among a group of women embodying Islamic virtues. Affect and embodiment are crucial prerequisites of these techniques aimed at developing a particular religious subjectivity. Meyer (2006, 2009) has demonstrated how the embodiment of particular sensory regimes shapes the receptiveness of the body and mind for particular religious experiences. Hirschkind (2006) argues that listening to recorded sermons is a disciplining exercise that creates sensibilities and modes of moral receptiveness aimed at moral self-improvement.

The training programmes for *Hizmet* followers have similar goals and follow similar disciplining trajectories. In explaining the proper attitude of Muslims under global conditions, Gülen refers to the 'ideal human':

> These new people will be individuals of integrity who, free from external influences, can manage independently of others. No worldly force will be able to bind them, and fashionable-ism will cause them to deviate from their path. Truly independent of any worldly power, they will think and act freely, for their freedom will be in proportion to their servant-hood to God. Rather than imitating others, they will rely on their original dynamics rooted in the depths of history and try to equip their faculties of judgment with authentic values that are their own. (Gülen 2010, 81)

Gülen argues that his message is different from that of many other religious public figures around the world because he himself engages with modernity. He claims to present an Islamic treatise that genuinely touches on the global and universal principles of Islam by opening up to others. Gülen (2010, 89) states that the ideal Muslim 'is sensitive to the dignity and honor of other people as they are their own. They do not eat, they feed others. They do not live for themselves; they live to enable others to live.' These moral obligations can only be applied when learned and embodied through disciplining techniques and training of the body and mind. Much of what Gülen proposes refers to the so-called 'Golden Generation'. It is an ideal image of the perfect Muslim engaging with Islamic traditions and modernity in a new way (Kuru 2003).

An analysis of Gülen's cosmopolitan theology and the ways that it is taught and reproduced must take into account the complex relationship between the political-historical and theological roots of the movement, the vastly changing characteristics of the followers, and the particular pedagogics applied in all kinds of educational settings. I will therefore first describe the central principles of Gülen's world view and teachings that are most relevant to the theme of cosmopolitanism and global responsibility. Then I will address the question of how the movement teaches its followers to seriously engage with an ethnically and religiously diverse world and how this bears on the modes of teaching.

Fethullah Gülen's message: a this-worldly moral appeal

Although Gülen does not use the term cosmopolitanism in his writings, he refers to the idea. A central creed in Gülen's teachings is 'peaceful coexistence' (of people with different convictions and backgrounds) and 'dialogue'. These themes appear in much of the written material produced by the movement. *Hizmet* (service) is one of the central maxims of Gülen's teachings. It denotes 'activist pietism' (as opposed to escapist mysticism). It refers to social service grounded in a religiously inspired ideology and the need to serve and be responsible to God by making the world better through active engagement, not withdrawal (Özdalga 2000; Esposito and Yilmaz 2010). This attitude requires, according to Gülen, a notion of global connectedness and moral responsibility towards an increasingly diverse world and its inhabitants (Kurtz 2005; Carroll 2007). *Hizmet* is this-worldly activity to create a more rational and ethically better society and requires a particular consciousness, civic responsibility and concomitant competences. This is much in line with what Weber ([1930] 1989) has referred to as 'in-worldly asceticism'.

Gülen's writings are an intriguing mix of esoteric often cryptic theological reflections and contemplations, and an appeal to the world. There are basically three clusters of concepts to be found in the writings of Gülen and his followers that constitute the core creed of human interdependence: (1) tolerance, love and compassion; (2) dialogue, peace-building and coexistence; and (3) responsibility, civility and citizenship. Although these concepts belong to the standard discourse of many global organizations such as Amnesty International, the United Nations or the World Peace Forum, Gülen integrates them in his theological world view and explains them as Islamic principles. There is also logic in the sequence of these clusters when translating them into Islamic reasoning. In Gülen's (1994) philosophy, the first cluster constitutes the essence of Islam, but under modern global conditions the call to love and tolerance becomes a difficult task to accomplish because we live in such a complex world inhabited by strangers. So it is the duty of every Muslim to train oneself to develop an attitude of responsibility and to apply it towards non-Muslims. Gülen (2010, 198) emphasizes the crucial role of education in this process: 'As ignorance is the most serious problem, it must be opposed with education, ... Now that we live in a global village, education is the best way to serve humanity and to establish a dialogue with other civilizations.'

A very crucial and intriguing aspect of Gülen's teaching is what I would call his reverse rhetorical frame. Instead of the commonly used logic of starting with divine doctrines and theological principles of Islam, he first sets out to explain the 'problems of humankind' in our contemporary world. He then teaches how to cope with the challenges of living under these conditions. Finally he demonstrates that a tolerant and cosmopolitan attitude has deeply spiritual underpinnings. Islam, according to Gülen, is in essence a cosmopolitan religion (Saritoprak 2005, 421). Understanding and appreciating this essence requires training and disciplined learning.

The clusters of concepts are connected to one another through *Hizmet*, which not only denotes service to God, but also implies civility and dedication in one's work and in society. Gülen expects Muslims to submit to God, to pray and to perform daily Islamic duties, but if one sticks to these normative and ritual obligations without understanding their implications, it will not lead to a growing awareness and sensitivity to the world around us. It will certainly not be enough to act in a responsible way towards others and to recognize the diversity in the world. In 2010, Gülen published the book *Toward a Global Civilization of Love and Tolerance*. It is a compilation of earlier writings and provides a comprehensive overview of his central concerns. Today it is one of the most cited works of Gülen, particularly among non-movement members. I will use the book to further explain Gülen's cosmopolitan theology.

The book starts with general, universal statements about the basic properties of human beings. In the next part Gülen translates these universals to God's creation and shows how these universals are in fact part of God's plan. It is, however, the task of the individual human being to understand the difference between simple love for others and love for others through the love for God (Gülen 2010, 15). It is the individual responsibility of every Muslim to understand this important difference and to act accordingly. In the section on tolerance and forgiveness, Gülen argues that tolerance is the human capacity to forgive other people's mistakes. Implicitly he refers to non-Muslims as the 'others'. Dialogue, which is a central theme in the book, is the bridge between love, on the one hand, and responsibility and civility, on the other. Dialogue is an important tool for dealing with the complexity and diversity of a global world. It forms the basis of democracy, according to Gülen (2010, 77–78; see also Yavuz 2013, 181). Gülen also stresses that loving those who have different opinions and convictions is not at all easy but it is the task of every Muslim to learn how to overcome intolerance and to treat others with respect. It should be emphasized that Gülen does not promote cultural relativism in the sense of cultural neutrality. There is a moral hierarchy between different world views and faiths and Gülen argues from a position of moral superiority and benign sovereignty of Islam. But Muslims have to engage with a world inhabited by people of different faiths and convictions, which is more than sheer tolerance. His moral appeal rests on the moral obligation to acknowledge this diversity and to learn to interact with diverse communities. Towards the end of the book, in a chapter titled 'Global perspectives', Gülen presents a spiritual message that is very reminiscent of a New Age creed:

With the blessings and beneficence of God, we are going to do our best to help this breeze of tolerance and dialogue to continue blowing; it is a breeze that has only recently begun to blow and it shows a tendency toward spreading over the entire world. (Gülen 2010, 257; see also Hunt and Aslandogan 2006).

What makes Gülen's ideas different from those of other Islamic preachers? An appeal for compassion and love or a call for responsibility is in itself not unique in Islamic traditions. Many Sufi traditions centre on the idea that the bond between God and individual believers is the basis for how human beings should relate to one another (see e.g. Werbner 2003). Also the emphasis on learning and training is not very unique. One thing that differentiates Gülen from his counterparts is the translation of the message of compassion into a concrete programme for action and the particular techniques of teaching, training and discipline to be practised by his followers. To grasp these differences more fully, we have to look to the roots of the movement, the ways in which Gülen's message is disseminated, and how internal communal cohesion is intertwined with external engagement.

Islam in Turkey: origins of the Gülen movement

The Gülen movement is a branch of the *Nurcu* movement, which was founded by the charismatic Islamic scholar Saidi Nursi (1873–1960). Nursi was of Kurdish descent born in the eastern Turkish town of Bitlis. After a few years of training in a local *medrese (religious school)*, he went to the city of Mardin at the border with contemporary Syria where he soon became known for his profound knowledge of both Islamic and Western sources. He acquired a group of disciples who called him *Bediüzzaman* (the marvel of his time) (Dumont 1986; Mardin 1989; Yavuz 2009). In Istanbul, where he arrived at the turn of the century, he became one of the leading figures in discussions about the future of the Ottoman Empire. He was a strong advocate of a unified Islamic empire including Muslims of different ethnic backgrounds (Turner and Horkuc 2009). Although Nursi formally supported the new republican government in 1923, he remained critical towards Atatürk's secularization policies. He withdrew from active politics and concentrated on his theological work.

Nursi is best known for his magnum opus *Risale-i-Nur* (*The Message of Light*). It is a series of texts and comments on the sources of Islam. Only in the 1950s, shortly before his death, did Nursi give permission to his followers to translate the *Risale* into different languages and in Latin script. This had a tremendous effect on the dissemination of his thinking. Today, the written and online spoken version of the *Risale* constitutes one of the central works studied by the followers of Gülen. Nursi has sometimes been described as the 'Spinoza of the Islamic world'. Many of Gülen's followers argue that the many parallels between Nursi and Spinoza are also found in Gülen's teachings (Celik 2010, 125–133). Nursi encouraged his followers to study science of whatever nature because it is the only way to understand God's creation. Nursi referred to the 'machinery of nature' as one of the mysteries of God's creation (Mardin 1989, 214), but he also emphasized study as an indispensable method to understand how humankind is connected to the divine universe. 'Trust', which is a central theme in Nursi's writings on the relation between God and human individuals, denotes the responsibility that people have towards God's creation (Turner and Horkuc 2009, 60).

The roots of Nursi's teachings, and consequently those of the Gülen movement, are found in the mystical traditions of Islam. Nursi, however, always rejected the term 'mystical order' as a characteristic of the movement. It did not have the close-knit organizational structure and type of leadership typical of Sufism. Nursi considered himself a messenger of God's word and works and not a spiritual leader (Van Bruinessen 2010). Many of the learning techniques and disciplining practices employed by the organizations and institutions of the Gülen movement are rooted in the teachings of Nursi and the way that he interacted with his followers. However, Nursi concentrated on teaching and learning and eventually renounced the world. Gülen translated this into a this-worldly programme for action.

Gülen was born in a village in the eastern province of Erzurum in 1941, in a Turkish area surrounded by Kurdish villages. He was unofficially trained as a religious priest and became familiar with the teachings of Nursi. In 1966, Gülen started his career as a religious teacher when he was appointed by the Turkish Directorate of Religious Affairs in the western city of Izmir, generally known as the 'least religious city of Turkey'. Here he developed his own interpretation of Nursi's legacy and founded one of the two branches of the *Nurcu* movement. His work, amid a rather militant secular part of the Turkish population, taught him to communicate religious views in ways that attracted the interest of people beyond the narrow confines of his followers. It was in those years that Gülen gradually laid the basis for his movement.

In the 1980s, Gülen became an important figure in the reform programmes and a prominent *alim* (religious scholar) in Turkey. Gülen maintained close ties with Prime Minister Özal and his *Motherland-party* (ANAP) when it came to power in 1983. The ANAP initiated radically new economic policies that opened up Turkey to the world and did away with the Kemalist protectionist policies that had guided previous economic programmes. These reforms led to the emergence of the so-called 'Anatolian tigers', a new middle class supporting neo-liberal economic transformation while promoting a conservative religious way of life (Yavuz 2009, 77). It created new economic opportunities; a participatory, political system; the 'mediatization' of politics and new forms of communication networks; and an emphasis on civil rights. An important aspect of Gülen's political philosophy was the emphasis on strengthening civil society and the opening up of the public sphere. He considered freedom of expression for a multiplicity of religious and political voices an essential prerequisite for a sound political environment (Turam 2007). 'Dialogue' soon became a keyword in Gülen's philosophy. It was based on the idea that Muslims had to develop the proper attitude to act in a society that consists of a multitude of voices and opinions. In those years, Gülen successfully established schools and other educational facilities. They provided general education, but they also constituted the institutional setting for teaching his ideas.

Gülen became one of the prominent opponents of the successful Islamic Welfare Party (RP), led by Necmettin Erbakan. In 1995, the RP became the biggest political party in Turkey. Erbakan became prime minister and many observers predicted that Turkey would become a 'second Iran' and 'slide back into fundamentalism'. Erbakan mounted several symbolic acts, such as shifting his diplomatic focus away from the West towards the Islamic world. On 29 February 1997 a 'silent military coup' served as a kind of ultimatum – Erbakan resigned. A series of measures were taken to weaken organized Islam and strengthen state control. Although Gülen was in no way involved in political activities, the military also launched a campaign against him and he decided to move to the USA, where he currently lives and works.

Within the RP, tensions between competing factions ultimately produced a split. Many young members left to found the *Justice and Development Party* (AKP), under the leadership of the current Prime Minister Erdogan. The AKP adopted a political and economic programme reflecting Turkey's changing political and social circumstances at the end of the 1990s. When it was clear that the AKP had distanced itself from Erbakan supporters, Gülen publically announced his support. According to political observers, his backing was decisive in the AKP's landslide victory in the 2002 general elections.

From his new residence in the USA, Gulen was able to attract funding from a wide variety of sources and build a commercial empire with newspapers, television stations and other media (Ebaugh 2010, 83). As a result, the movement became more visible and attracted the attention of the young urban middle class who hitherto had been uninterested in Islamic ideas. During the 1990s and, in part, due to the growing number of highly educated young followers, the movement shifted its attention away from the conservative lower class to the new middle class. Since many of its new followers held more cosmopolitan world views, Gülen moved away from nationalist rhetoric towards a more moderate individualist notion of Islam. It also furthered the impression that the AKP was heavily supported by Gülen. At the same time it should be noted that the evolution of *Hizmet* in the past two decades from conservatively nationalist into a moderate, more open and more cosmopolitan movement reflects the fundamental changes that took place in those two decades.

In recent years, tensions grew between Gülen and the leadership of the AKP, notably Erdogan himself. These tensions amounted to a real clash in mid-2013. The Gülen movement was accused of infiltrating and undermining the Turkish state, while Gülen argued that Erdogan had completely abandoned his initial ideals of clean and democratic politics.

Teaching *Hizmet*

Cosmopolitanism, according to Calhoun:

> is not merely a matter of cocktails or market ebbs and flows. It's what we raise in those who read novelists from every continent, or in the audiences and performers of world music; it's the aspiration of advocates for global justice and the claim of managers of multinational businesses. (Calhoun 2008, 109)

This refers to a particular attitude, a mode of 'being in the world'. Cosmopolitanism is more than a mobile way of life; it can generate global civic awareness implying an evaluative and normative imperative that must be learned. Leichtman and Schulz (2012, 2) use the term 'vernacular cosmopolitanism' to describe a 'particular set of practices, a disposition, and a specific cultural and social condition that allows Muslims to inhabit the contemporary world'. This ethos and the active engagement of Muslims in the contemporary complex world are at the core of *Hizmet*'s educational activities.

As I have indicated, under the influence of the changing economic, social and cultural landscape in the 1980s, Gülen gradually shifted his focus from Turkish politics towards a more open and internationally oriented agenda. The success of the movement in the 1990s and its spread beyond Turkish borders resulted in a sharp increase in the dissemination of the movement's teachings in different languages. After the fall of the Soviet Union in 1989, Gülen concentrated on extending his network to the newly independent Turkic states in Central Asia. It was the first step to extend his influence beyond Turkey's borders. In the course of years, the movement founded schools and institutions elsewhere in Asia, Africa, Europe and the Americas. The more *Hizmet* expanded globally, the more it became necessary to develop a message that included non-Turkish followers and to shift the teaching focus to inter-religious dialogue. These developments are crucial to understand Gülen's cosmopolitan theology.

Today the movement produces a dazzling amount of books, articles, course materials, pamphlets, speeches, podcasts and blogs. The movement publishes the newspaper *Zaman*, the biggest newspaper in Turkey, with regional versions in more than ten different languages. They have their own broadcasting company *Samanyolu* and an extensive network of publishing houses across the world. The efficiency and tight organization of its network of schools also explains its success (Agai 2007). The movement has also published an impressive body of texts including comments, interpretations and explanations, not only from Gülen himself, but from a number of his disciples and from people sympathetic to Gülen's views. All of these materials aim to reach a broad audience through a variety of rhetorical styles ranging from formal preaching to scholarly analysis. Each contains a clear message of redemption, hope and promise.

In addition, numerous seminars, conferences and lectures focus on the implications of Gülen's teachings for humankind. In many countries, the movement works in close cooperation with secular universities. In several places, it has funded endowed professorships. In this way, it has embedded itself in a broad variety of institutional settings (Ebaugh 2010). There are also a growing number of scholarly articles addressing Gülen's efficacy and appeal. In addition to these written sources, the movement operates educational institutions across the world that organize lectures, discussion meetings, conferences and training (Agai 2007; Van Bruinessen 2010). All these activities are well-known modes of knowledge transfer accessible to the general public.

The comparatively large number of documents in English, together with the inclusive appeal of Gülen's message, has helped shape the image of the movement as an open, loose network of people inspired by the teachings of their spiritual leader. As I indicated earlier, this openness has often been perceived as contradictory to the strong discipline and dedication demanded from active participants. As Kurtz (2005, 373) points out: 'It is the paradoxical fusion of intense faith commitment with tolerance towards others that characterizes the double character of the movement.' However, the inextricable connection between global outreach and internal discipline constitutes the backbone of Gülen's cosmopolitan theology. Being active in the world as envisioned by Gülen does not occur by itself; it requires insight, hence training and discipline.

This inner circle of students is mainly recruited from among highly educated young people. Once a member, they follow a trajectory of intense learning and reflecting on a wide variety of sources of knowledge. Although they must study Islamic sources and perform religious duties as part of their training, they are also always required to complete a successful educational career in society. Students learn through intellectual and physical exercises. The genuine source of spirituality and ethics is not the sermon of the imam in the mosque or the teacher in the *medrese*, but the collective building of schools, the encouragement of economic enterprises, and the mental disposition that makes possible these acts (Özdalga 2000, 95). Spirituality and religious learning make sense only in combination with active participation in society. The training and teaching activities take place at so-called *yurts* (boarding school) or *dersane* (dormitory). Their goal is to produce a new generation of young Muslims that is capable of participating fully in a contemporary world (Van Bruinessen 2010). The type of people that the movement claims to create, the *altin nesil* ('Golden Generation'), is not just a remote ideal; it is the goal of the intensive training programme. Salvation and mental tranquility are accomplished through the performance of good deeds and through working to create a better world.

A true dedication to the universal message of Islam thus requires commitment and intensive training and learning that only a selected group of students is able to accomplish. According to Gülen, *Hizmet* is a never fully accomplished: as soon as the work is done, new tasks are waiting. *Daha yok mu Allah'im?* (Is there nothing more to be done, my God?) is one of the catchphrases of the movement. This produces a certain hastiness and restlessness in the mind, but it also makes followers of the limits of life itself. According to Gülen, life has to be lived to its limits, both in a spiritual sense and by doing good in the world. Gülen formulated five principles to proper conduct in this world that combine a do-it-yourself attitude with submission and discipline: (1) critical attitude towards all statements; (2) be aware of the limits of life in this world; (3) keep good friendship alive; (4) never stop reading; and (5) be aware of the fact that you share your dedication to the cause with a select group of people.

Hizmet is thus an attitude that must be acquired through a disciplining process. It involves the complex interaction between (open, universal and rational) knowledge acquisition and embodiment and self-discipline. The inner circle of the movement must train their bodies and minds through daily rituals growing out of the movement's Sufi origin. Rather than focusing on formal legal sources such as the Koran, Hadith and *fikh*, a dedicated member disciplines his or her mind and body through prayer, rituals, and reading and studying Gülen's work. Understanding the true nature of God's word and its implications for one's life requires a sufficient level of receptiveness and sensibility. Acquiring divine knowledge is thus a matter of training.

An elaborate system of mentorship and social control is organized around a programme of personal reflexive routines performed in addition to the regular Islamic daily rituals. Every member must take part in the regular *sohbet*, a partly ritual, partly educational meeting with fellow students and guided by a mentor. The constituent elements of a *sohbet* session demonstrate the complex and unique interplay between cognitive reflection, confessional introspection and ritual repetition with the aim to develop a particular habitus. In addition to these sessions, practitioners must also keep a daily diary, a *cetele* in which daily duties are recorded. These routines and tasks are discussed individually with a mentor or with the head of the boarding house (Van Bruinessen 2010; Yükleyen 2012).

The most successful members become *abis* (elderly brothers) or *ablas* (elderly sisters), which enables them to mentor new members. The complex and demanding training programme that is required should, however, not divert the student from being actively engaged in the world and being a successful member of society. Rather, one should learn to understand that ignoring either aspect of life makes the other meaningless. The religious doctrine of the Gülen movement mainly revolves around the idea that a strong dedication to God and a disciplined and ascetic private life enhances societal and public success and activism. Members must focus on both personal and social transformation. A life in accordance with God's will creates responsible and valuable citizens and thus a better society. Serving God and serving the world are not two mutually exclusive duties, according to Gülen. Rather, active engagement with the world emanates from a proper reading of God's word.

Conclusion

The *Hizmet* is a global Islamic movement in more than one sense. Its current success across the world and its rapid growth is not just the result of an effective media strategy to spread its message using modern technology. Gülen is more than a 'technically globalized Muslim intellectual'. The strong, well organized local cadres and networks of schools and educational activities enable not only the spreading of Gülen's word, but also its translation to local conditions and circumstances. The combination of these two global modes of dissemination, together with the ever-widening reach of the movement, gives rise to a particular religious discourse and practice that successfully addresses the global conditions under which an increasing number of Muslims in the world live. It provides them with a sense of self and the necessary tools with which to address that reality in meaningful way. Members are trained to develop competencies with clear cosmopolitan underpinnings: 'a good Muslim embraces the world'.

The transformation of the *Hizmet* movement from an esoteric Sufi community into a global religious movement with a strong outwardly oriented message brings to light an intriguing development about the way that the movement is perceived. With its rising prominence, *Hizmet*'s ever-widening and inclusive message stands in stark contrast to its esoteric and secretive ways of knowledge production and the sectarian and closed character of its inner circles. This contradiction has often been depicted as Gülen's double face and the esoteric practices he espouses as some sort of 'cover up'. The more young members of *Hizmet* have become visible in society and the more they are actively engaged in it, the more this double image is depicted as a way to detract attention from Gülen's 'Islamist agenda' to turn Turkey into an Islamic state (see e.g. Koç 2008; Sharon-Krespin 2009).

However, as I have argued in this article, to pose these two aspects of *Hizmet* as contradictory or as the outer and inner face of the movement misses the point. First, it assumes that the transformation of the movement from the 1980s onwards was a strategy of deception that did not reflect Gülen's intentions. Rather, this transformation took place in response to the movements changing position within the Turkish political landscape and the changing demography of the rank and file of *Hizmet*, which also transformed Gülen's vision of Islam in the contemporary globalized world. Second, it is the combination of these two qualities that constitute the core characteristic of *Hizmet*. Being a responsible Muslim and a responsible citizen in this world are similar qualities. Openness and inclusiveness on the one hand and strong internal discipline and exclusiveness on the other reinforce rather than contradict each other, not least because only those who successfully combine a virtuous life with an active this-worldly attitude are considered members of the 'Golden Generation'.

Note

1. For a discussion of Appiah's views, see Hoesterey (2012).

References

Agai, Bekim. 2007. "Islam and Education in Secular Turkey: State Policies and the Emergence of the Fethullah Gülen group." In *Schooling Islam: The Culture and Politics of Modern Muslim Education*, edited by Robert Hefner and Muhammed Qasim Zaman, eds., 149–171. Princeton: Princeton University Press.

Appiah, Kwame. 2006. *Cosmopolitanism. Ethics in a World of Strangers*. New York: W.W. Norton.

Asad, Talal. 1993. *Genealogies of Religion. Discipline and Reason of Power in Christianity and Islam*. Baltimore, MD: John Hopkins University Press.

Boender, Welmoet. 2007. *Imam in Nederland. Opvattingen over zijn religieuze rol in de samenleving* [Imam in the Netherlands. Visions about His Religious Role in Society]. Amsterdam: Bert Bakker.

Bowen, John. 1993. *Muslims through Discourse*. Princeton: Princeton University Press.

Bowen, John. 2010. *Can Islam be French*. Princeton: Princeton University Press.

Calhoun, Graig. 2008. "Cosmopolitanism in the Modern Social Imaginary." *Daedalus* 137 (3): 105–114.

Carroll, Jill. 2007. *A Dialogue of Civilizations. Gülen's Islamic Ideals and Humanistic Discourse*. Somerset, NJ: The Light.

Celik, Gürkan. 2010. *The Gülen Movement. Building Social Cohesion through Dialogue and Education*. Delft: Eburon.

De Koning, Martijn. 2008. *Zoeken naar een zuivere Islam* [Searching for a Pure Islam]. Amsterdam: Bert Bakker.

Dumont, Paul. 1986. "Disciples of the Light. The Nurju Movement in Turkey." *Central Asian Survey* 5 (2): 33–60. doi:10.1080/02634938608400542.

Ebaugh, Rose. 2010. *The Gülen Movement. A sociological Analysis of a Civic Movement Rooted in Moderate Islam*. New York: Springer.

Eickelman, Dale, and Jon Anderson, eds. 2003. *New Media in the Muslim World. The Emerging Public Sphere*. Bloomington: Indiana University Press.

Epel, Gilles. 2000. *Jihad: Expansion et Déclin de l'Islamisme* [Jihad: Expansion and Decline of Islamism]. Paris: Editions Gallimard.

Esposito, John, and Ihsan Yilmaz, eds. 2010. *Islam and Peacebuilding. Gülen Movement Initiatives*. New York: Blue Dome Press.

Foucault, Michel. 1993. "About the Beginnings of the Hermeneutics of the Self." *Political Theory* 12 (2): 198–227. doi:10.1177/0090591793021002004.

Gräf, Bettina, and Jakob Skovgaard, eds. 2009. *Global Mufti. The Phenomenon of Yusuf al-Qaradawi*. New York: Columbia University Press.

Gülen, Fethullah. 1994. *Kalbin Zumrut Tepeler* [The Sapphire Peaks of the Heart]. Izmir: Pirlanta Kitap Serisi.

Gülen, Fethullah. 2010. *Toward a Global Civilization of Love and Peace*. Somerset, NJ: Tughra Books.

Hefner, Robert, and Muhammad Qasim Zaman, eds. 2007. *Schooling Islam: The Culture and Politics of Modern Muslim Education*. Princeton: Princeton University Press.

Hirschkind, Charles. 2006. *The Ethical Soundscape. Cassette Sermons and Islamic Counterpublics*. New York: Columbia University Press.

Hoesterey, James. 2012. "Prophetic Cosmopolitanism: Islam, Pop Psychology and Civic Virtue in Indonesia." *City and Society* 24 (1): 38–61. doi:10.1111/j.1548-744X.2012.01067.x.

Hunt, Robert, and Yilmaz Aslandogan, eds. 2006. *Muslim Citizens of the Globalized World: Contributions of the Gülen Movement*. Somerset: The Light and IID Press.

Koç, Handan. 2008. "Gülen cemaatinin ilk ve en saf halkası? [The First and Most Pure Prayer Groups of the Gulen Community]" *Express*, 89. Kasim 2008. Accessed December 2013. http://www.habervesaire.com/haber/1269/.

Kurtz, Lester. 2005. "Gülen's Paradox: Combining Commitment and Tolerance." *The Muslim World* 95: 373–384. doi:10.1111/j.1478-1913.2005.00100.x.

Kuru, Ahmet. 2003. "Changing Perspectives on Islamism and Secularism in Turkey: The Gülen Movement and the AK Party." Unpublished Document.

Leichtman, Mara, and Dorothea Schulz. 2012. "Introduction to Special Issue: Muslim Cosmopolitanism: Movement, Identity, and Contemporary Reconfigurations." *City and Society* 24 (1): 1–6. doi:10.1111/j.1548-744X.2012.010 64.x.

Mahmood, Saba. 2005. *Politics of Piety. The Islamic Revival and the Feminist Subject*. Princeton: Princeton University Press.

Mardin, Şerif. 1989. *Religion and Social Change in Modern Turkey. The Case of Bediüzzaman Said Nursi*. New York: State University of New York Press.

Meyer, Birgit. 2006. *Religious Sensations. Why Media, Aesthetics and Power Matter in the Study of Contemporary Religion Inaugural Lecture*. Amsterdam: VU University.

Meyer, Birgit. 2009. *Aesthetic Formations. Media, Religion, and the Senses*. New York: Palgrave MacMillan.

Özdalga, Elisabeth. 2000. "Worldly Asceticism in Islamic Casting: Fethullah Gülen's Inspired Piety and Activism." *Critique: Critical Middle Eastern Studies* 9 (7): 83–104.

Roy, Olivier. 2002. *Globalized Islam. The Search for a New Ummah*. London: Hurst.

Saritoprak, Zafer. 2005. "An Islamic Approach to Peace and Nonviolence: A Turkish Experience." *The Muslim World* 95: 413–427. doi:10.1111/j.1478-1913.2005.00102.x.

Sharon-Krespin, Rachel. 2009. "Fethullah Gülen's Grand Ambition: Turkey's Islamist Danger." *Middle East Quarterly* 16 (1): 55–66.

Turam, Berna. 2007. *Between Islam and the State*. Stanford: Stanford University Press.

Turner, Colin, and Hasan Horkuc. 2009. *Said Nursi*, London: I.B. Tauris

Van Bruinessen, Martin. 2010. *De Fethullah Gülenbeweging in Nederland* [The Fethullah Gulen Movement in the Netherlands]. Utrecht: Universiteit Utrecht.

Weber, M. 1930/1989. *The Protestant Ethic and the Spirit of Capitalism*. London: Unwin Hyman.

Werbner, Pnina. 2003. *Pilgrims of Love: The Anthropology of a Global Sufi Cult*. London: Hurst.

Yavuz, Hakan. 2009. *Secularism and Muslim democracy in Turkey*. Cambridge: Cambridge University Press.

Yavuz, Hakan. 2013. *Toward an Islamic Enlightenment. The Gülen Movement*. Oxford: Oxford University Press.

Yilmaz, Ihsan. 2005. "State, Law, Civil Society and Islam in Contemporary Turkey." *The Muslim World* 95: 385–411. doi:10.1111/j.1478-1913.2005.00101.x.

Yilmaz, Ihsan, ed. 2007. *Peaceful Coexistence. Fethullah Gülen's Initiatives in the Contemporary World*. London: Leeds Metropolitan University Press.

Yükleyen, Ahmet. 2012. *Localizing Islam in Europe*. Syracuse: Syracuse University Press.

Zaman, Muhammad Qasim. 2009. "The Ulama and Contestations on Religious Authority." In *Islam and Modernity: Key Issues and Debates*, edited by Muhammad Khalid Masud, Armando Salvatore, and Martin van Bruinessen, 206–237. Edinburgh: Edinburgh University Press.

Globalizing forms of elite sociability: varieties of cosmopolitanism in Paris social clubs

Bruno Cousin and Sébastien Chauvin

This article examines the cultivation of transnational connections, cosmopolitanism and global class consciousness among members of elite social clubs in Paris. Drawing from interviews with members, it compares how – according to their respective characteristics – various social clubs promote different kinds of bourgeois cosmopolitanism, while rejecting the more recent internationalism of upper-middle-class service clubs such as the Rotary. Each club's peculiar ethos, practice and representations of social capital are related to the features of competing clubs through relations of mutual symbolic distinction; for example, some clubs emphasize the 'genuineness' of links while stigmatizing others for the accent they put on utility. The varied forms of cosmopolitanism that they promote partly replicate these logics of distinction, eliciting struggles over the authenticity or inauthenticity of transnational connections. Yet, clubs also oppose each other according to the unequal emphasis that they place on international ties per se, which creates a competing axiology within the symbolic economy of social capital accumulation.

Since the Middle Ages, European elites and upper classes have always considered themselves more cosmopolitan than other social groups.[1] Such self-representations resulted in part from geographical mobility and inter-cultural contacts fostered by specific institutions, for example: networks between nobiliary courts, between monasteries and, later, universities; linguae francae and common scholarly languages; the circulation of cultural goods; commercial partnerships, political alliances and norms of exogamy; the *peregrinatio academica* and the Grand Tour (Elias [1969] 1983; Duby [1981] 1983; Le Goff [1984] 1992, 2001; Braudel [1979] 1992; Chartier 1994; Black 2003).

In the contemporary period, several works in the sociology and anthropology of cosmopolitanism have emphasized how different experiences of intercultural or transnational inclusiveness are linked to specific social positions, connections, sociability practices, institutions, world views and shared narratives (see e.g. Hannerz 1990; Tarrius 2000; Lamont and Aksartova 2002; Wagner 2007a; Calhoun 2008; Duyvendak 2011; Glick Schiller, Darieva and Gruner-Domic 2011; Ossman 2013). They have found that cosmopolitanism and the promotion of cosmopolitan values does not preclude class exclusiveness, boundary work, or a concern for distinction. Indeed, the version of cosmopolitanism most valued by globalized elites often goes together with the stigmatization of the less mobile and the differently connected. Yet, structural and symbolic relations *between the different forms* of cosmopolitanism (or internationalism) have never been systematically studied, aside from the ways in which rich 'expats' distance themselves from poor 'immigrants' (Green 2008). At the top of the social ladder, several recent qualitative studies analyse the transnational sociability of the 'old money' upper class (Saint Martin 1993; Pinçon and Pinçon-Charlot [1996] 1998; Wagner 2007b), expatriate families of international executives and managers working for large corporations (Wagner 1998; Beaverstock 2002, 2005), free-moving professionals as a Europeanized upper middle class (Scott 2006; Favell 2008)[2] and exchange students in the EU Erasmus programme. But, although some of this work makes comparisons between these groups, they seldom address the ways in which framing processes and practices of symbolic boundary making result in distinct international identities and resources, nor how these identities connect with logics of social domination between fractions of the upper class.

Adopting a Bourdieusian perspective, the pioneering work of Anne-Catherine Wagner briefly underscores how recently acquired skills and dispositions towards 'international' cultural capital are looked down upon as superficial, inauthentic and too explicitly instrumental by those who inherited them through early socialization (Wagner 1998, 117–123, Wagner 2004, 136). Cosmopolitan heirs see their own comprehensive experience of growing up within a transnational and multilingual environment as more truly and deeply transformative than any formal learning provided by national school systems or company training programmes.

However, if Wagner gives a clear hint of the ways that certain international *cultural* competences and knowledge can be legitimized or delegitimized from another social position, she does not explore how international *social* capital – both transnational connections and local acquaintances with foreigners – can also elicit symbolic struggles over its more or less distinctive character. These dynamics of distinction are our focus here: by pointing rival experiences of international sociability, we contribute to the study of the symbolic economy of social capital among the upper classes (Cousin and Chauvin 2012). Our argument draws on data collected on Paris elite social clubs: since 2010, we conducted twenty-one in-depth interviews among the members of the city's five clubs – Jockey Club, Nouveau Cercle de l'Union, the Travellers, Automobile Club de France and Cercle de l'Union Interalliée[3] – supplemented with ethnographic observation and archival research. These institutions of sociability were chosen for three reasons: (1) because their explicit function is to manage and develop the social capital of their members; (2) because they contribute significantly to the boundary work among different parts of the upper classes (Pinçon and Pinçon-Charlot 1989, 193–252; Khan 2012, 371); and (3) because social clubs are still key in the internationalization of the bourgeoisie, a point that has been overlooked in the literature until now.[4]

How elite clubs foster class-based cosmopolitanisms

The Jockey is the most aristocratic, legacy-based and patrilineal of all Parisian social clubs;[5] its members acknowledge these characteristics very openly. Its primary raison d'être is to perpetuate the links between the male descendants of the nineteenth-century French conservative ruling class, whose belonging to the elite goes back even further. Refined Frenchness is proudly cultivated as part of a restricted group identity and through its special relation with national history. However, its members often come from families traditionally at ease in several countries, within Europe and on both sides of the Atlantic, where their undisputable nationally rooted prestige serves as a guarantee of their social status.

For instance, Alexandre, a thirty-eight-year-old Jockey member from a ducal house who ranked among the Peers of France, was raised in one of the wealthiest *arrondissements* of Paris, where he attended a private elementary school named after his family and then several secondary institutions around the country, which familiarized him with many regions of France. He explained:

> I am very French, by my origins, by my family, by my education, by my environment, by the people I see, by many things. (…) Thus I really have an origin: my blood and my origins are from somewhere. My roots.

Yet, he went abroad right after graduating (with difficulty) from high school. He studied business economics for two years in Brussels, six months in Madrid and six months in Dublin, was drafted into the military for a year, and came back to Paris for his fourth year of college. At the same time, he spent every summer interning in the USA, which led to a job in New York City after graduation. He lived there for twelve years, working successively as a derivatives trading support associate, a financial adviser, the chief financial officer and partner of an advertising agency, and finally for a hedge fund managing investments for many wealthy European aristocratic families, whose founder was himself a Jockey Club member. He also obtained a finance MBA from New York University, an MA in financial mathematics from Columbia, and US citizenship. He now considers the USA his adoptive country.

The Great Recession, however, brought him back to France, where he created his own financial company, which he located in Geneva. At the time of the interview, his clients were mainly French, Swiss, Luxembourg-ish, Belgian and British, while the financial products he distributed were managed in the USA. Therefore, he was living between Paris and Geneva and spending one week every month in New York where he was still a partner in the advertising agency.

When in New York, Alexandre is a regular at the Knickerbocker Club, with which the Jockey (like the Nouveau Cercle de l'Union (NCU) and the Travellers) has a reciprocal arrangement, and where he can entertain his US acquaintances. In fact, even though he lives mainly in Europe, he spends much more time at the 'Knick' than at the Jockey. He became familiar with the Jockey by going to private parties (*rallyes*) organized at the club for teenagers of the upper class. Today, he often meets male family members and old family friends there, which makes him feel a strong sense of belonging. Yet, the club is primarily a way for him to get direct, easy access to the sociability of the traditional East Coast elite of the USA. More generally, as Alexandre insisted:

> When I travel, my first reflex is to check if there isn't a reciprocal club in the city I will be visiting: New York is of course an easy example... London is another one... When I visit Brussels, there is the Cercle du Parc where I go from time to time, to have lunch or just to pass by. And that's very pleasant. It's pleasant because you feel at home. (...) Another anecdote: I was having lunch [at the Jockey] with my dad; we were sitting at a table with two people I didn't know. We talk business a bit – not really about work, just about industry in general and how things are going... – and one of them asks me: "So you travel a lot... are you going somewhere soon?" I tell him yes, that I'm leaving for Brazil in two weeks to spend two weeks there, for business and for pleasure, and I tell him that I don't know the country. And he tells me: "Well, wait: one of my nephews is in Rio, so if you go to Rio, get in contact with him!" I got in contact with him by email, and we saw each other almost every day! Thus I would say there is this notion of quasi-instantaneous affinity.

In a similar manner, a financial analyst and board member of the Jockey told us how much he appreciates frequenting the Circolo della Caccia, which is located in the Borghese Palace in Rome, both for the 'quite exceptional environment' and for the feeling of social familiarity and comfort that he experiences every time he goes there. The Jockey Club and its international network of partner clubs indeed promotes class-based cosmopolitanism – 'But this is not shutting ourselves off from the world,' clarified Alexandre. 'It is merely, at certain moments, having a world in which we can be among ourselves.'

Among the other Parisian social clubs, the Nouveau Cercle de l'Union (NCU) is most like the Jockey. It grew out of several consecutive mergers during the nineteenth and twentieth centuries, the last of which occurred in 1983 between the Nouveau Cercle and the Cercle de l'Union – itself established in 1828 with the explicit Anglophile motivation of strengthening the links between French and British elites and importing to Paris a form of sociability already typical of London's high society (Gmeline 2003). Today, however, the NCU and its 500 members are less attached to their aristocratic heritage than Jockey members. In addition to offering the traditional leisure activities of the French conservative upper class (equestrian sports, hunting, golf and gaming), the NCU also promotes cultural and scholarly exchanges. Many of its members are bibliophiles, and interest in history and international relations is a long-standing characteristic of the club. It awards two non-fiction literary prizes for history and autobiography every year, has strong connections with the Société d'Histoire Diplomatique and its journal, and a second history prize awarded by a jury mainly composed of foreign ambassadors. Two recent presidents of the NCU, René de La Croix de Castries and Gabriel de Broglie, were illustrious amateur historians and fellows of the Académie française. A few other members also belong to the Institut de France (the most prestigious French honorary society, which includes the Académie). More generally, while the majority of NCU affiliates are part of the business world, it also has the highest share of diplomats,[6] top civil servants, journalists and writers among its members. The NCU's proximity to culture and diplomacy leads its members to perceive the world through a more intellectual frame than the other clubs, even though, for many of them, cosmopolitanism primarily results from social intercourse with professional intercultural mediators (who are sometimes asked to give formal presentations). A thirty-six-year-old audit manager of a multinational corporation told us:

> When you have great ones, when you have Renaud Girard, a distinguished reporter at *Le Figaro*, when you have a Jean Bothorel, who is at *L'Express*, it is interesting to discuss with this kind of persons, rather than to chat with the old aristocrat who has an old estate and keeps lamenting, saying "we were a great family and now everything falls into pieces," with his three cows... He's a kind fellow, but one must live in the world! (...) I prefer a hundred times talking with Renaud Girard. Each time he gives a conference there I go, and it is captivating! He brags a bit, but that's part of his character... and I prefer having tea with him.

The cosmopolitanism of NCU members grows less out of their pre-existing private and personal connections than at the Jockey and is more often institutionally mediated. Indeed, its members are affiliated with multiple organizations, fostering class-based internationalism according to a variety of criteria. For instance, several NCU members – qualified descendants of the French commissioned officers who served during the American Revolutionary War – are also members of the USA's oldest patriotic society: The Society of the Cincinnati (and can therefore automatically be affiliated with the less socially selective Sons of the American Revolution).[7] More importantly, *all* NCU members also belong to the much broader Cercle de l'Union Interalliée (CUI, most often referred to as l'Interalliée), originally established in 1917 as a social and dining club where Parisian elites could socialize with the officers and prominent figures of France's allies during the First World War.

The NCU members we interviewed criticized the size, lower selectivity, lack of conviviality, and mixed gender make-up of l'Interalliée (whose membership reaches over 3,300 persons). They complained that these characteristics do not really allow CUI affiliates to be personally known by the staff and to know each other, and that it is therefore 'more like a luxury hotel than a real social club'. Since the NCU is housed on a dedicated floor of CUI's building, it is literally a club within a club. Its members, however, often appreciate this two-tiered organization, as it allows them to combine the more intense and distinctive sociability of the smaller institution with the larger infrastructure and services offered by the other, which include a network of 136 partner clubs in twenty-nine countries (Pinçon and Pinçon-Charlot 2007, 233). In contrast, the NCU affords a more restricted choice of seventeen partners that it considers to be its equals.[8] A thirty-six-year-old antique dealer explained:

I travel a lot for work, and when I'm abroad I stay at the clubs. I find it nicer and less impersonal than the hotel. Our advantage is that since we are the oldest club in Paris and the fanciest – with the Jockey – we have equivalences with the fanciest. In London I know almost all of them, and in New York... But I try to stay at the same ones as much as I can: for sure in New York the best is the Knickerbocker, and in London I generally stay at Boodle's, because it is really our matching club, and otherwise I sometimes stay at the Athenæum... Because, what's not bad with the fact that we are automatically members of the Interalliée is that we also benefit from all its partnerships, and they are countless! I think it is probably the club in the world with the highest number of reciprocal agreements... But it doesn't position itself in the same way we do: we look for *the best* club in a certain country, while they look for quantity. In New York they might have five or six partners; and we absolutely do not! And, true, in London we have two equivalences, but in London they are a lot of gentlemen's clubs: we have Boodle's, which is the fanciest after White's, but White's doesn't have reciprocal agreements with anybody. And we have the Athenæum because it is the intellectual one.

Thus, NCU members see their club as playing a distinct role in the diversified set of tools that they use to manage their social capital and international connections, including their families, informal circles of friends, professional and inter-professional networks, exclusive clubs that act as status markers, and more integrated clubs that broaden their reach.

Compared with the Jockey and the NCU, cosmopolitanism at the Travellers is even more explicit. The Travellers is class-based and elitist like the former two, but in a way that directly values professional status and promise, primarily in law and finance, in addition to high social origin. It promotes the international integration of a de facto Western upper class: the club was created in 1902 as a counterpart to its homonym in London, and still has reciprocal agreements almost exclusively with gentlemen's clubs in Europe and in the Americas.[9] However, more than any other Parisian club, its purpose is to foster *international* social capital among its members. As prescribed by the Travellers' regulations, around half of its 800 members hold foreign citizenship (alone or in addition to French nationality); the majority are British or American. Members are listed in a directory including their nationalities; several come from historic transatlantic families (like the de Gunzburg). Finally, the club has a special non-resident membership category for people living abroad. In contrast to other clubs that require residence in France, the Travellers supports their co-optation (for instance, George Soros is a member).

Moreover, just how much cosmopolitanism is valued and legitimized is evident in the Travellers' membership criteria. As opposed to the other Parisian social clubs, transnational mobility experiences and not being (only) French are seen here as intrinsically positive qualities, which partially compensate for one's lack of inherited social status. A thirty-seven-year-old lobbyist, who is a member of the Board of the Travellers and also a member of the Jockey, detailed:

> It is true that, among the young Americans whose parents were members of the Travellers, many now live in London or New York, and are members of affiliate clubs. Thus they have no real advantage in being members here. When you are a member of the Knickerbocker in New York, or of Boodle's or the Turf in London, if you come to France you can come here. (...) But we are very open to Americans or Englishmen who would work in Paris. Even if they are not members by family tradition. (...) In this respect it is very international, and it is especially open to international curriculums. Whereas we will tend to require family pedigrees from the pure French, someone who has a father or a mother who is American (or Austrian, or something else) will be very welcome at the Travellers, without us going to his home country to get information on his origins. (...) When you have decided to settle and to work in Paris even though you are completely American, it gives a dimension of open-mindedness, a culture: it is not open to everyone.

The contrast with the Jockey Club is clear. The latter changed its entry rules following the recent international controversy that arose when it admitted Baron Albert Frère, a self-made man and the richest man in Belgium,[10] who had been previously turned down by the Jockey's partner in Brussels. The Parisian club subsequently revised its admission policy to stress clear national prerogatives. Foreign candidates can no longer be considered for admission if they come from a country where the Jockey has a partner club but they are not already a member of it. As one board member explained, a man's reputation is better assessed in his country of origin.

The Travellers is also a place where members' international backgrounds get converted into status markers that are more identifiable and meaningful in the French context – in addition to providing access to Paris's high society. Many interviewees spoke of these processes of prestige translation. Nicholas, a thirty-nine-year-old dual citizen (one of his grandparents was French, the other three American), who lived back and forth between the USA and France until the age of twenty-two when he finally settled in France and then founded a trilingual family with his German wife, is now the chief executive officer of a financial communication company. When describing his academic background, he said:

> But who in France knows Brown? Or, even less: who knows Phillips Exeter Academy? (…) I am in France with a baggage that comes from the United States, but which does not mean anything in a French context. If I had been to Harvard, or perhaps Yale, this is transportable baggage that can cross the Atlantic and still mean something… But unfortunately for me, in the French context I have never benefited from the slightest advantage related to that, because they are in fact references that don't mean anything for anyone here. And that's precisely another interest of being at the Travellers: you are potentially facing people who… this, they know, and this evokes something for them. And thus, it makes an extra link (…), a common reference.

Conversely, since the club is well known by part of the world's upper class, some respondents described inviting foreign business partners or customers to the Travellers to signal that they belonged to the French establishment. In a similar way, while abroad, members of the Travellers can simultaneously assert class belonging and display a cosmopolitan habitus by taking advantage of reciprocal agreements and bringing local acquaintances to prestigious clubs that many have never entered, although they are in their own country.

Finally, with more than 2,000 members, the Automobile Club de France (ACF) is Paris's largest gentlemen's club. It was founded in 1895 both as a private club and as a public organization for the promotion of automobiles. Today its building still contains the headquarters of the Fédération Internationale de l'Automobile, the organization that oversees motorsports at the global level. However, activities related to cars are now a separate, rather marginal aspect of the ACF's life: only 200 of its members are part of an internal subgroup of car enthusiasts (which requires a distinct application). This contrasts with the ubiquity of automobiles – especially antique ones – in the ACF's interior decoration and strategies of self-representation, which celebrate French auto industry pioneers, thereby serving as an enduring source of symbolic capital for the club and its members.[11] Indeed, as a social club, the ACF aims to bring together industrial elites at the national level.

Its centripetal orientation distinguishes it from the more outwardly oriented clubs interested in transnational relations. The ACF is particularly open to entrepreneurs from all over France who visit Paris regularly for business – whether as guests of Parisian members or as members themselves. It is also the only social club in Paris to have a reciprocal agreement with a club in another French city: the Club de l'Union, in Lyon. But until recently it had no agreement with clubs in New York (in 2007, its only partner in the USA was in Chicago) and, although its members often say how much they admire English traditions of masculine sociability, such Anglophilia often grows out of literature and reputation rather than out of intimate experience with London's clubs. Besides, that very few ACF members are foreigners and that very few foreigners grace its doorstep is not judged a problem: despite its 10,000 square metres, ACF's building does not have bedrooms; infrequent guests stay in rooms at the Jockey Club, thanks to an agreement between the two institutions.

Indeed, although many ACF members do have some international experience and connections, they develop them mostly through other institutions of sociability. Thus Basile, a thirty-six-year-old lobbyist for a national business association, expanded his network in the Americas thanks to the Association France-Amériques; and Louis, a thirty-four-year-old private banking manager who belongs to an old family of automobile industrialists, regularly stays at the Knickerbocker Club in New York because he is also a member of Paris's Travellers.

Varieties of cosmopolitanism and the symbolic economy of social capital

Beyond the question of cosmopolitanism and transnational ties addressed in this article, our wider research on social and service clubs (Cousin and Chauvin 2010, 2012) draws attention to how each club frames social capital and defines the best way to accumulate it. Our findings suggest that because members face unequal conditions for accumulating resourceful connections, symbolic hierarchies and competition arise over how each group represents their social capital and over the criteria each uses to connect their members with each other.

At the Jockey Club and at the NCU, social capital is generally inherited and conceived as collective patrimony. Its consolidation and mobilization are framed as 'natural', spontaneous and disinterested, with no other direct purpose but leisure, and as private as a familial relation can be. Thus the Jockey and the NCU differ from other institutions of (upper-)middle-class sociability such as the Rotary and other service clubs (Camus-Vigué 2000), which recruit members based on their professional status and present themselves as useful tools for social network engineering. The Travellers and the ACF occupy an intermediate position, combining a valorization of legacy and strong ties within a select upper class with meritocratic and utilitarian preoccupations.

Thus, in line with the conflict between '*mondain*' (effortlessly elegant) and '*docte*' (scholastic) relations to *cultural* capital identified by Bourdieu ([1979] 1984, 70) among French elites, we observed disagreements over the best way of acquiring and managing one's social capital, which grow out of the unequal and different ways through which it is acquired by members of these different organizations. Social club members, especially ones at the Jockey and the NCU, almost unanimously scoff at what they consider the artificiality, inherent vulgarity and pushiness of the Rotary. Often without even being asked, they feel the need to point out that Rotary clubs (and other service clubs) are something 'totally different' from social clubs and 'have nothing to do' with them. Denis, the sixty-four-year-old president of the CUI, former president of the NCU and long-time member of the Jockey, told us of one of the most egregious cases of misinformed journalism he ever had to correct – when the writer described him as belonging to the Rotary. Jockey and NCU members also regularly invoke the Rotary as a foil against which they contrast good practices from bad, as when they criticize other clubs for being too utilitarian and network-driven. In a more light-hearted manner, they emphasize the less aristocratic origin of Travellers and ACF members, and their (supposedly laborious) strategies of social capital accumulation, by nicknaming them respectively '*les Travailleurs*' [the Workers] and '*les Garagistes*' [the Mechanics].

Our inquiry into the symbolic boundaries marked by different social actors to categorize sociability and friendship practices (Lamont and Molnár 2002) required that we combine classical approaches to social capital as a set of individual resources (e.g. Bourdieu 1980; Portes 2010) with the relational approach to symbolic struggles deployed in *Distinction*, thus integrating two parts of Bourdieu's ([1979] 1984) theoretical framework in a new way.

But how do the distinctions that clubs make over how social capital should be accumulated and used map onto the varieties of cosmopolitanism we described earlier? For the most polarized positions, the two logics of differentiation essentially blend. For instance, the members of the five

Paris social clubs see the Rotarians and their more than 1,000 French clubs as a multitude of local and provincial elites, whose claim to be 'international' –based on the coordinated activities, exchange programme and official principles of Rotary International (Goff 2008) – gets short shrift because, from their perspective, Rotary clubs are not even in touch with France's centralized national power structure and therefore cannot pretend to transcend it. Additionally, they criticize the artificiality of an organization that implements the exact same model of sociability everywhere around the world and which prospects and plans international contacts mainly as group activities and discovery tours (and not primarily to facilitate its members' pre-existing cosmopolitanism and transnational mobility, as in social clubs).[12]

However, when elite social clubs contrast themselves *with each other*, logics of distinction do not just revolve around the authenticity or artificiality of international connections. Indeed, clubs also disagree over how important it is to have international connections in the first place and whether the club should be a place for accumulating them. As a consequence, oppositions between different forms of social capital are only reflected in those between different forms of cosmopolitanism to a limited extent. In fact, the latter space of struggle partly subverts the former and therefore makes it more complex. For example, although Travellers' interviewees who cannot belong to the Jockey or the NCU sometimes acknowledge that their lack of aristocratic legacy and inherited social capital is a handicap, most insist that their own 'international profile' fits with their club's view that cosmopolitanism is an intrinsic virtue. This alternative positive interferes with the generic axiology pitting 'genuine' experiences of social capital against 'interested' ones. In fact, the Travellers can be more business oriented in part because it is more international. As it is often difficult to define with precision the family background of a foreign applicant who grew up outside of France, the club relies more on his professional position to establish his social status. In addition, as many foreign members do not have family or old friends at the Travellers, they are less likely to consider the club as a natural extension of their closest circle of relations and see it more as a work-related space.

In response to the symbolic positioning of the Travellers, members of the ACF – which, as we saw, is the least internationally connected of all Paris social clubs – try to minimize the importance of cosmopolitanism and having contacts abroad altogether. 'Not everybody wants to have lunch next to an American banker,' summarized one ACF member referring to the Travellers. As for the NCU, its members reframe internationalization as a qualitative rather than a quantitative issue, stressing the importance of acculturation. From this perspective, of course, the learned cosmopolitanism and intercultural mediators of the NCU appear particularly legitimate, while the 'spontaneity' of the Jockey and the 'international openness' of the Travellers can both be stigmatized as superficial and simplistic. The latter is even blamed for calling people international who do not deserve it. As one thirty-six-year-old member of NCU put it: 'There you find any dick who is a small lawyer in an English or American firm: that's his life accomplishment! [*bâton de maréchal*].'

Conclusion

This article examines the cultivation of transnational connections, cosmopolitanism and global class consciousness among members of Paris social clubs. It compares how these clubs promote different kinds of upper-class cosmopolitanism, while differentiating themselves from the more recent internationalism of upper-middle-class service clubs such as the Rotary. Games of distinction between clubs around the greater authenticity of their competing forms of social capital take place both at a general level and around *international* social capital in particular (as some transnational connections are stigmatized as more superficial or utilitarian than others). Yet, clubs also disagree about the value of international ties per se, thus activating a competing axiology within the symbolic economy of social capital accumulation.

While theorists such as Kwame Anthony Appiah (2006) present globalized (upper-class) cosmopolitanism as potentially universal, Craig Calhoun (2008) suggests that we need to empirically examine who gets to be cosmopolitan with ease and who struggles to achieve it or remains uninterested. Yet, far from marking linear differences that could be measured along a single scale of cosmopolitanism, various material conditions and social institutions foster different sorts of cosmopolitan inhabitation of the world, also within the upper class. These differences not only arise from unequal degrees of exposure and sensitivity to global interdependence (Beck 2006) but can be produced by dynamics of symbolic competition between class fractions.

Revealing the class infrastructure of contemporary cosmopolitanisms also frames the question of global citizenship in new ways. As a diacritical political institution, citizenship has always drawn a line between the included and excluded within a given territory (Bosniak 2006). Thus, the rising notion of global citizenship invites us to scrutinize the new hierarchies that it may imply. By exacerbating people's unequal access to mobility and transnational ties based on their unequal resources and their positions within contemporary capitalism, globalization potentially shifts civic hierarchies to the world level (Sassen 2006). Besides nationality and economic capital, social capital plays a key role in determining how well individuals can access global resources and status, and in the shaping of their cosmopolitan representations and practices.

The feeling of being world citizens does not preclude that of belonging to the globalized class of the privileged, nor does it prevent the explicit cultivation of *entre-soi* – as Michel Pinçon and Monique Pinçon-Charlot designate the in-group togetherness that they identified as the main class-reproduction strategy of the French bourgeoisie. France's elite global citizens do not feel any less distinct from the global poor than they feel distinct from the French poor when thinking of themselves as French citizens. This is especially true considering that the international *entre-soi* cultivated by Paris's social clubs through their partner clubs 'around the world' steadily persevere in a Western (and white) ethnic tropism, ignoring the elites of the Global South, including the ones of France's former colonial empire, as much as it ignores at home the members of the French elite from ethnic minority backgrounds. Furthermore, as we saw, elitism and cosmopolitanism can go hand in hand: cosmopolitanism itself can function as a source of distinction from the less mobile or less broadly connected – whether the lower classes or those within the upper class who owe their legitimacy to more strictly national resources.

Moreover, in-depth interviews with members of social clubs suggest that the global elite, far from being obsessed with distinguishing itself from the world's masses, can be mostly preoccupied with emulation and competition among privileged peers and subgroups. Further research is needed to measure how much these internal dynamics of class distinction contribute to the internationalization of elites, and to explore the consequences of these processes for the emergence of global cosmopolitan values within and beyond the upper classes.

Acknowledgements

We would like to thank Apostolos Andrikopoulos, Mabel Berezin, Rogers Brubaker, Jan Willem Duyvendak, Shamus Khan, Michèle Lamont, Peggy Levitt, Ashley Mears, Ann Morning, Jules Naudet, Pál Nyíri, Susan Ossman, Rachel Sherman, Tommaso Vitale, Roger Waldinger and anonymous reviewers of *Ethnic and Racial Studies* for their comments on the previous versions of this article.

Notes

1. In this article, when no further specification is given, we use the terms 'cosmopolitan' and 'cosmopolitanism' in a limited and non-moral acceptation. They refer to travelling abroad, being part of and cherishing a network of international contacts, displaying intercultural ease, and feeling at home in different countries. It is therefore a quality and world view that does not necessarily have to do with the sharing of universalistic or egalitarian values. This restricted sense, which is already documented in Diderot and d'Alembert's *Encyclopédie* and texts by many English-speaking figures of the Enlightenment, is also – nowadays – the usual meaning of the French word '*cosmopolite*'.

2. Other monographs focus on the cosmopolitanism fostered by the activity and the professional sociability of specific cultural producers or mediators: artists,

writers, academics, foreign correspondents, diplomats, United Nations personnel, and so on.

3.   All interviews (except one with an American interviewee) were conducted in French, at one of the clubs (ten interviews out of twenty-one), at the apartment of the interviewee (two), at his office (three), at our faculty office in Paris (five), or by phone (one). Except for this latter, which lasted only twenty minutes, the duration of each interview ranged between one hour and three hours twenty-five minutes. Interviewees were recruited through chain referral. All the quotes in the article were translated by us.

4.   Although this article focuses on the French case, the theory of elite social capital that we deploy and some of the findings we present here were first outlined in a previous study conducted in Italy, on Milan's social clubs and most prestigious Rotary clubs (Cousin and Chauvin 2010).

5.   Today, 97% of the 1,100 Jockey members come from aristocratic families, with the consequence (related to the distinct professional traditions between the French upper classes) that many of them work in the financial services, in real estate, or as top civil servants, diplomats and sometimes as entrepreneurs. On the other hand, the great families of the industrial bourgeoisie are almost not represented in the club, whose aristocratic component has progressively expanded since its creation in 1834 (Mension-Rigau 2003).

6.   In addition to the presence of many French diplomats among the regular members, the (male) ambassadors of several countries are honorary members of the NCU for the duration of their appointment in Paris.

7.   In comparison, the members of the Travellers – whose families generally entered the elite later but often studied in the USA – tend to be more involved in alumni associations (those of Harvard, Yale, Princeton, Columbia and Stanford are particularly active in Paris).

8.   The Jockey Club also has less than twenty reciprocal agreements, all of them with clubs located outside France that it considers its foreign counterparts. This special attention to international social equivalence was particularly patent when, after 150 years of partnership with London's Turf Club, the members of the Jockey recently considered that Turf's social selectivity had declined (among other reasons, because it was keeping with the tradition of facilitating the admission of racehorse owners). They therefore decided to find an additional – more appropriate – British partner, and made an agreement with Boodle's.

9.   'We are open to the world, but it does not mean we are open to all cultures,' a thirty-three-year-old investment banking manager told us, also evoking the fact that, in all Paris social clubs (although a little less at the Travellers and at the ACF), not being of Catholic origin – and, more broadly, not being Christian – can be an obstacle to admission. For instance, only 2% of ACF members have African or Asian surnames: mainly Sephardic, but also often Lebanese (or Persian). They generally come from other national bourgeoisies that moved to Paris after major geopolitical events – either the end of the French colonial empire, the Lebanese civil war or the Islamic revolution – and almost never from upwardly mobile labour migration.

10.   It is interesting to note that A. Frère's candidacy to the Jockey Club had been sponsored by French American David René de Rothschild, current head of the tricentennial international banking empire known today as the Rothschild Group

and of one of the world's most prominent cosmopolitan families (which is also among the few belonging traditionally to the Jockey despite not being Catholic).
11. In a similar way, interviewees from the ACF stressed the fact that the swimming pool of the club and the metal structure that tops it were designed by Gustave Eiffel.
12. Rotary International has a very meticulously planned 'Friendship Exchange Program' (based on a *Rotary Friendship Exchange Handbook*) designed to create *new* international connections between its members, and whose goals include 'learn[ing] how [Rotarians'] vocations are practiced in other parts of the world', 'observ[ing] new customs and cultures' and 'promot[ing] an appreciation of cultural diversity worldwide' (2009 edition, 1).

References

Appiah, Kwame Anthony. 2006. *Cosmopolitanism. Ethics in a World of Strangers.* New York: Norton.

Beaverstock, Jonathan V. 2002. "Transnational Elites in Global Cities: British Expatriates in Singapore's Financial District." *Geoforum* 33 (4): 525–538. doi:10.1016/S0016-7185(02)00036-2.

Beaverstock, Jonathan V. 2005. "Transnational Elites in the City: British Highly-skilled Inter-company Transferees in New York City's Financial District." *Journal of Ethnic and Migration Studies* 31 (2): 245–268. doi:10.1080/1369183042000339918.

Beck, Ulrich. [2004] 2006. *The Cosmopolitan Vision.* Cambridge: Polity. [In German].

Black, Jeremy. 2003. *Italy and the Grand Tour.* New Haven, CT: Yale University Press.

Bosniak, Linda. 2006. *The Citizen and the Alien. Dilemmas of Contemporary Membership.* Princeton: Princeton University Press.

Bourdieu, Pierre. [1979] 1984. *Distinction. A Social Critique of the Judgement of Taste.* Cambridge, MA: Harvard University Press. [In French].

Braudel, Fernand. [1979] 1992. *Civilization and Capitalism. 15th–18th Century (Vol. 2: The Wheels of Commerce; Vol. 3: The Perspective of the World).* Berkeley: University of California Press. [In French].

Bourdieu, Pierre. 1980. "Le capital social. Notes provisoires." *Actes de la recherche en sciences sociales* no. 31: 2–3.

Calhoun, Craig. 2008. "Cosmopolitanism in the Modern Social Imaginary." *Dædalus* 137 (3): 105–114.

Camus-Vigué, Agnès. 2000. "Community and Civic Culture: The Rotary Club in France and the United States." In *Rethinking Comparative Cultural Sociology. Repertoires of Evaluation in France and the United States*, edited by Michèle Lamont and Laurent Thévenot, 213–228. Cambridge: Cambridge University Press.

Chartier, Roger. [1992] 1994. *The Order of Books. Readers, Authors, and Libraries in Europe between the 14th and 18th Centuries.* Cambridge, MA: Polity Press. [In French].

Cousin, Bruno, and Sébastien Chauvin. 2010. "La dimension symbolique du capital social : les grands cercles et Rotary clubs de Milan." *Sociétés Contemporaines* 77: 111–138. doi:10.3917/soco.077.0111.

Cousin, Bruno, and Sébastien Chauvin. 2012. "L'économie symbolique du capital social. Notes pour un programme de recherche." *Actes de la recherche en sciences sociales*, no. 193: 96–103. doi:10.3917/arss.193.0096.

Duby, Georges. [1981] 1983. *The Knight, the Lady and the Priest. The Making of Modern Marriage in Medieval France*. Chicago, IL: The University of Chicago Press. [In French].

Duyvendak, Jan Willem. 2011. *The Politics of Home: Belonging and Nostalgia in Western Europe and the US*. Basingstoke: Palgrave Macmillan.

Elias, Norbert. [1969] 1983. *The Court Society*. Oxford: Blackwell. [In German].

Favell, Adrian. 2008. *Eurostars and Eurocities. Free Movement and Mobility in an Integrating Europe*. Oxford: Blackwell.

Glick Schiller, Nina, Tsypylma Darieva, and Sandra Gruner-Domic. 2011. "Defining Cosmopolitan Sociability in a Transnational Age. An Introduction." *Ethnic and Racial Studies* 34 (3): 399–418. doi:10.1080/01419870.2011.533781.

Gmeline, Patrick de. 2003. *De l'Union au Nouveau Cercle... le Nouveau Cercle de l'Union. 175 ans d'histoire*. Paris: Éditions de Venise.

Goff, Brendan B. 2008. "The Heartland Abroad: The Rotary Club's Mission of Civic Internationalism." PhD diss., Department of History, University of Michigan, Ann Arbor.

Green, Nancy L. 2008. "La migration des élites. Nouveau concept, anciennes pratiques?" *Les Cahiers du Centre de Recherches Historiques* no. 42: 107–116. doi:10.4000/ccrh.3434.

Hannerz, Ulf. 1990. "Cosmopolitans and Locals in World Culture." *Theory, Culture & Society* 7 (2–3): 237–251. doi:10.1177/026327690007002014.

Khan, Shamus R. 2012. "The Sociology of Elites." *Annual Review of Sociology* 38(1): 361–377. doi:10.1146/annurev-soc-071811-145542.

Lamont, Michèle, and Sada Aksartova. 2002. "Ordinary Cosmopolitanisms. Strategies for Bridging Racial Boundaries among Working-Class Men." *Theory, Culture and Society* 19 (4): 1–25. doi:10.1177/0263276402019004001.

Lamont, Michèle, and Virág Molnár. 2002. "The Study of Boundaries in the Social Sciences." *Annual Review of Sociology* 28 (1): 167–195. doi:10.1146/annurev.soc.28.110601.141107.

Le Goff, Jacques. [1984] 1992. *Intellectuals in the Middle Ages*. 1st revised French ed. Oxford: Blackwell.

Le Goff, Jacques. 2001. *Marchands et banquiers du Moyen Âge*. 9th ed. Paris: Presses Universitaires de France.

Mension-Rigau, Éric. 2003. "La noblesse et le Jockey club." In *Élites et sociabilité en France*, edited by Marc Fumaroli, Gabriel de Broglie, and Jean-Pierre Chaline. Paris: Perrin.

Ossman, Susan. 2013. *Moving Matters. Paths of Serial Migration*. Redwood City: Stanford University Press.

Pinçon, Michel, and Monique Pinçon-Charlot. 1989. *Dans les beaux quartiers*. Paris: Seuil.

Pinçon, Michel, and Monique Pinçon-Charlot. [1996] 1998. *Grand Fortunes. Dynasties of Wealth in France*. New York: Algora [In French].

Pinçon, Michel, and Monique Pinçon-Charlot. 2007. *Les Ghettos du Gotha. Comment la bourgeoisie défend ses espaces*. Paris: Seuil.

Portes, Alejandro. 2010. "Social Capital." In *Economic Sociology. A Systematic Inquiry*, edited by A. Portes, 27–47. Princeton: Princeton University Press.

Saint Martin, Monique de. 1993. *L'Espace de la noblesse*. Paris: Métailié.

Sassen, Saskia. 2006. *Territory, Authority, Rights. From Medieval to Global Assemblages*. Princeton: Princeton University Press.

Scott, Sam. 2006. "The Social Morphology of Skilled Migration: The Case of the British Middle Class in Paris." *Journal of Ethnic and Migration Studies* 32 (7): 1105–1129. doi:10.1080/13691830600821802.

Tarrius, Alain. 2000. *Les nouveaux cosmopolitismes. Mobilités, identités, territoires*. La Tour d'Aigues: L'Aube.

Wagner, Anne-Catherine. 1998. *Les nouvelles élites de la mondialisation. Une immigration dorée en France*. Paris: Presses Universitaires de France.

Wagner, Anne-Catherine. 2004. "La mondialisation des dirigeants économiques." In *Le retour des classes sociales. Inégalités, dominations, conflits*, edited by Paul Bouffartigue, 125–139. Paris: La Dispute.

Wagner, Anne-Catherine. 2007a. *Les classes sociales dans la mondialisation*. Paris: La Découverte.

Wagner, Anne-Catherine. 2007b. "La place du voyage dans la formation des élites." *Actes de la recherche en sciences sociales*, no. 170: 58–65. doi:10.3917/arss.170.0058.

Pirate cosmopolitics and the transnational consciousness of the entertainment industry

Olga Sezneva

As cultural texts, music and movies generate transnational publics united by shared identities and tastes. As objects of economic value, they fall under the juridical protection of global intellectual property institutions. These institutions aspire to produce their own version of a global citizen *qua* the responsible consumer. This paper argues that illegal copying and distribution have a capacity to forge new transnational affiliations. At the same time, they are subject 'abjection' by the apparatus of copyright enforcement. Focusing on the acts of semantic enclosure that such enforcement produces, the paper concludes that 'policing' has been increasingly mobilized as a path to becoming 'global citizen', thus reducing possibilities for the development of a critical, pluralistic subjectivity commonly termed 'cosmopolitan'.

Everyone knows the wickedness or inventiveness – choose your epithet – of First World college students and Third World bazaar store-holders, armed with digital technology, who are liberating text from its owners. Securing copyright, charging rent, running distribution, choking off new market entrants – all the standard monopoly-capital norms of Hollywood are compromised by these tricksters. Copying content has never been easier. The MPA finds new ways each week to fantasize about the revenue lost to teenagers in US dorms and merchants in Chinese malls. (Miller 2007, 1)

Introduction: reading cosmopolitanism through piracy

The audience and fans of today's pop stars span the world and connect individuals in ways that are disconnected from specific national territories and cultures. Given the transnational nature of the entertainment industry's iconic objects – 'the international hit' and 'the blockbuster' – this is hardly surprising. The rise of the customary practice – also globally shared – of illegal copying and distribution is equally predictable: extensively 'hyped' and therefore desired, these same cultural artefacts are not always easily accessible through legal channels. The entertainment industry has gone to extreme lengths to prevent illegal copying, but the challenges are serious. Responding to them requires not only advances in legal instruments and digital rights management technology, but also cultivation of a particular awareness of the private ownership of a creative product that extends the bond of reciprocity between consumers and producers across national and other divides.

This special issue explores how cosmopolitan subjects are actually 'made', what they believe in and how their beliefs impact their actions by examining different – including potential – sites of global citizenship creation. This particular paper takes on copyright as its subject and examines it as a strategic site for the development of a theory of cosmopolitanism. The global expansion of intellectual property regimes (IPR) opens a new thematic area for the inquiry into the relationship between popular culture and cosmopolitanism.

Many have claimed that the flows of images and information about distant places and people are enough to encourage reflexive distancing from the immediate and the familiar: as long as cultural commodities introduce a disposition to 'think, feel, and imagine beyond existing group boundaries'[1] (Beck in Saito 2011, 126), their circulation has the potential to create a cosmopolitan public. The circulation of music and movies gives rise to new forms of subjectivity simply because, as cultural texts, they have the capacity to shape individuality as they intensify humans' semiotic productivity, enhance social sharing of meaning, experience and self-styling, and lead to making new cultural artefacts (Fiske 1992; see also Hansen 1994; Warner 2002). When they circulate internationally, they become particularly potent in exposing nationals to cultural differences.

However, this semiotic functioning of cultural artefacts is countered by another logic – that of economics, the realization of cultural products' monetary value. IPRs have come to play the role of 'containment' mechanisms (Sezneva and Chauvin 2014), which has increased the costs of (re)production and limited the scope of circulation of cultural artefacts. Furthermore, one imperative in the current rolling out of copyright globally has been the formation of a shared global consumer consciousness in its support – what one might call copyright law's own 'transnational public'. As a result, cultural flows today are organized by at least two 'cultures of circulation' (Gaonkar and Povinelli 2003; Aronczyk and Craig 2012): the semiotic and the economic.

This article is based on a review of the literature on intellectual property studies and the author's own work on emerging media markets in Russia. It examines how and to what extent the semiotic capacity of artefacts as cultural texts interacts with the juridical aspirations of global intellectual property institutions. Whereas the former may be generative of transnational publics, the latter strive to produce a global citizen *qua* the responsible consumer. These universalistic aspirations, however, systematically fail to materialize, as is evidenced by the rampant rates of illegal copying worldwide. These illegal practices need to be understood not only in relation to intellectual property, but also – and crucially so – as a response to the condition under which semiotic functioning of the social text simply cannot be realized. That is, the formation of a transnational public is constricted by acts of forging the transnational consumer.

To reflect on the relationship between illegal copying – 'piracy' – and copyright, I follow Peter Nyers' (2003) work on political subjectivity of the asylum seeker from which he develops the theory of 'abject cosmopolitanism'. I utilize this notion in my own analysis of media piracy to demonstrate how illegal copying and distribution have a capacity to forge new transnational affiliations, but at the same time become subject to political exclusion. I then focus on the acts of semantic enclosure defined by Jacques Rancière (2001) as 'policing'. In conclusion, I argue that intellectual property enforcement acting as 'policing' results in a reduction of possibilities for the development of a critical, pluralistic subjectivity commonly termed 'cosmopolitan'.

Pirate cosmopolitics

Bruno Latour (2013, 457) wrote in his critique of Ulrich Beck's sociology of cosmopolitanism that:

> Cosmopolitans may dream of the time when citizens of the world come to recognize that they inhabit the same world, but cosmopolitics are up against a somewhat more daunting task: to see how this "same world" can be slowly composed.

This claim resonates with what a number of scholars have already pointed out: cosmopolitanism evolves not only out of certain aesthetic and ethical orientations, but also from conflict, political contention and other insurgent practices; furthermore, those insurgent practices themselves often cut across borders and produce their own forms of cosmopolitanism (Calhoun 2010; Brennan 1997; Cheah 1998).

It is useful to recall here the insight of Breckenridge, Pollock and Bhabha (2002, 6) that cosmopolitans today are often the disgruntled 'victims of Modernity' failed by 'capitalism's upward mobility'. Building on this observation, Peter Nyers (2003) employs the figure of the asylum seeker refracted through the theory of cosmopolitanism to uncover a critical potential contained in the subject position 'abject migrant'. Playing on the mutually exclusive semantics of 'abjects' standing for someone being jettisoned and 'cosmopolitan' as someone 'belonging to the world', Nyers suggests that by acting politically, the asylum seeker challenges traditional notions of political community and citizenship. Subject 'to violent detachment' either due to the politics in the country they flee or the deportation regime they arrived into, the asylum seeker raises a possibility that 'cosmopolitanism's high value' of the polity that they seek to join may nonetheless rely on 'a relationship with an abject non-value for its condition of possibility' (Nyers 2003, 1073).

In the way similar to that in which the immigration regime converts the asylum seeker into a deportable, imminently excludible subject, the intellectual property regime exercises political violence to outlaw those who copy without permission. As I demonstrate in my paper, casting such acts as criminal and associating those who commit them with 'pirates' has been part and parcel of anti-piracy activism deploying the political strategy of abjection. This is where a comparison proves productive: if the abject migrant by exposing the logic of achieving the universal through exclusion turns a 'problematic cosmopolitanism for the abject' into a 'problematising cosmopolitanism of the abject' (Nyers 2003, 1075), then the abject 'pirate may' expose the political violence that accompanies the making of a global consumer (Dent 2012). The 'abject cosmopolitanism' of the pirate, consequently, may recast the image of the all-inclusive and sophisticated connoisseur of culture by attending to the diverse grounds of social experience from which one conceives of his or her cosmopolitan alternatives.

Equating the cosmopolitan pirate with the 'abject' also draws attention to the struggle over legitimacy between one culture of circulation over another, associated with unsanctioned copying. In his work on aesthetics, Jacques Rancière (2001, 2007) developed a theory of 'policing' that goes beyond law enforcement. 'Policing' for him refers to the practices of power that organize and sustain the social by constituting specific semantic universes and social and institutional networks. Notably, Rancière made an important distinction between policing and politicizing, placing the two at opposite ends of the spectrum vis-à-vis their effects on social order. In contrast to policing, politicizing creates spaces of dissent and contentious questioning – of the norms, tastes, dreams and imaginings of elites who sustain power hierarchies. I build on this extended perspective on policing and argue that the contemporary moment of anti-piracy activism represents an attempt to foreclose the semantic universe, by muffling dissenting voices as the noise. The 'cosmopolitan consumer order' effectively turns into 'cosmopolice'. A better understanding of practices and ideologies of unauthorized copying in the context of global inequality in return promises a step towards 'cosmopolitics', which sustains the diversity of cultures of circulation and open alternative paths to 'cosmopolitan virtue'.

The transnationalization of culture

Anthropologists, historians and sociologists have previously linked the shift towards professionalization in the production of culture to the rise of nation states and national forms of consciousness. Today, a huge portion of this production is created internationally and directed at transnational audiences, leading some scholars to argue that cultural goods circulating globally also operate as agents of cosmopolitanization (Beck and Sznaider 2010; see also Saito 2011). Indeed, the rates of transnationalization at the level of production are astonishing, and the global extent of movie and music markets testifies for an equally impressive inclusivity of aesthetic tastes no longer defined by the semantic codes of local culture. One of the main measures of success in the movie business, for example, is how well a film does at the worldwide box office. The desire to attract as large – and consequently as diverse – an audience as possible leads producers to use new universally appreciated encoding strategies. They affect character selection and creation and increase the number of action scenes and romances that have led to the segmentation of audiences by gender and age more than nationality (Kuipers and de Kloet 2009).

The transnationalization of entertainment has not been limited to plots and profits. It extends to production, financing, staffing and location scouting. Between 2004 and 2007, off-shore hedge funds located in the Cayman Islands provided $11 billion to finance Hollywood film production. In 2009, fundraising conducted by Dreamworks brought in $325 million of the $825 million from an Indian company (called Reliance Big Entertainment). Screen actors, directors, producers, writers, cinematographers, and costume, set and sound designers also come from around the world. International collaboration is becoming a regular part of British, French, Korean and Chinese film industries. *Chronicles of Narnia* had a British director, a producer from New Zealand, an Italian cinematographer and many Australians cast in various roles. The geography of production is equally global. Even the story of an escape from the Gulag, as in Peter Weir's film *The Way Back*, the overland passage of the fugitives from Siberia through the Himalayas to India, 'was shot in India, Morocco and at the former Bulgarian national film studio now known as Nu Boyana, with post-production undertaken in Australia' (Goldsmith, Ward, and O'Regan 2012, n.p.).

In the music market, the global appeal and reach of entire genres or individual songs has also increased. Singles charts compiled in the USA starting in 1940 by Billboard and in the UK in 1952 by NME can be seen as early indicators of the internationalization of rock and pop music, which was dominated by Anglo-American artists and industries (Stanley 2012; see also Regev 2013). The 1980s witnessed what at first appeared to be a counter-trend to Western domination, 'world music' – worldbeat, ethnopop, New Age, sono mondiale and *musique metisse* (hybrid music) genres.

The patterns of production of these genres closely followed the global mobility experienced by the musicians themselves. An artist of Caribbean descent, for example, might record most of his music in New York, where he hired two arrangers for the rhythm and bass who did not necessarily come from his country of origin. One might live remotely, for example in London; or the horn players might be based in Trinidad but the final mixing was done elsewhere (Guilbault 2001, 182–183).

The internationalization of music thus includes both production and consumption, but the latter does not always involve erasing the cultural specificity associated with a particular culture or place. The astronomical global success of Brazilian country singer Michel Teló in 2012, and the 'Gangnam Style' song that went viral in the same year, demonstrate how tradition and the seemingly narrow confines of national culture can generate a transnational allure. 'Gangnam Style' may be an ultimate example of something truly 'local' going extremely 'global'. A small area in Seoul, about the size of Manhattan and home to about 1% of the wealthy population, was popularized by Park Jae-sang, or PSY – singer, songwriter, rapper, dancer, record producer and television personality. Despite 'the apparent lack of overt popularity in South Korea', PSY has been given a 4th Class Order of Cultural Merit by the South Korean Ministry of Culture for 'increasing the world's interest in Korea' (Hiskey 2013).

What exactly is the status of such international hits, and what precisely is evidenced by the popularity of some music from the Global South has been debated. Do the examples such as world music or 'Gangnam Style' represent a disruption of 'the hegemonic order or assumed monolithic market logic' as Ian Chambers argues (1992), or a dramaturgy in which 'the subject becomes the Other of nobody', as Veit Erlman (1996, 486) conceives of it? Such discussions bring the issue of power differential into theories of cosmopolitanism that deal with cultural consumption. However, even those more attentive to the dynamics of inequality worldwide fail to address a more basic issue: how does access interact with and influence the formation of the transnational consciousness?

Global reach, local void

There is a certain popularized image of digitized contents – in the form of which most media products now circulate – flowing freely and unbound-edly: they can spread with unprecedented velocity making possible quasi-instantaneous transmissions from one geographic location to another without compromising their quality. Making access and use of cultural products ever easier, digitization and contemporary communication technologies are assumed to enhance transnational flows and ease the formation of cosmopolitan identities. However, the image is only true to limited extent, and there exists a far more variegated landscape of circulation.

World regions, for instance, are distinguishable by the dominant form of media embodiment: cassettes are popular in Mali and Nigeria, optical discs in China and Russia, while downloadable files are dominant in the USA and Europe. This implies an uneven availability of certain contents on legal markets. Since 2003–2005, streaming has taken on a much more prominent role in distribution, and the use of such services has grown rapidly as cheap devices and higher bandwidth connections have become more widely available. However, even among wealthy countries, streaming and downloading occur unevenly: median digital music file collections, for example, are significantly larger in the USA than in Germany, making evident regional variation in music consumption even within the industrial core (Karaganis and Renkema 2013). Outside it, such variations are even greater: the ability to stream requires a whole transmission infrastructure, which is why it is still limited to the Global North and select peripheral urban areas of the South, where bandwidth is noticeably improving. In Russia's two largest cities – Moscow and St. Petersburg – it appeared in 2007; in Mexico City, cable service primarily exists in middle-class neighbourhoods. The technical infrastructure in many developing economies has only recently become available and is still structured by income differences. This skews access towards more affluent social groups and major metropolitan areas.

Many distributors are reported to be uninterested in doing business in certain world regions because the costs are too high and popular access to licensed products is too limited. Major movie production studios and record labels target population groups with a specific – as a rule, relatively high – level of purchasing power that reflects a transnational 'middle-class' rather than a domestic-class structure. Not all regions of the world offer such a consumer base and many are excluded from legal distribution by inadequate pricing (Karaganis 2011). The resulting schism opens up a space in which the boundaries between legal and illicit have to be violated to make attainable music and movies that are otherwise inaccessible and which so many lower-middle- and working-class individuals throughout the world want desperately to consume

Technological development and pricing are not the only factors responsible for reliance of various publics on the 'pirate' channels of distribution. 'Windowing'– timing the release of a movie for different markets or segments of a market – allows businesses to keep different versions of the same product from competing with each other – for example, home videos always come after offerings in movie theatres. This drives up profits by offering the same content in a different media. Windowing protects economic value, but it also places cultural products into a time-limbo. Consider what happened in 2009 to Oscar-winning *Slumdog Millionaire* in India. The globally promoted movie was not released in India until five months after it was shown in the USA – an exceptionally long window of distribution. If the film grossed over $100 million internationally, it netted only $648,500 at the Indian box office because unauthorized distributors monopolized the market. Could this be a result of a low audience appeal of the movie itself? No. Its copies were widely circulating on DCTorrents and DesiTorrents, attesting to the film's considerable popularity. Rather, argue Liang and Sundaram (2011, 350), the global advertising campaign contributed to building the 'economy of anticipation' around the movie, but legal distribution lagged behind.

Finally, political censorship has been shown to have a strong effect on the accessibility of cultural goods. One historical example described by Mattelart (1994) and Kiriya (2012) is the Soviet Union, where cultural goods were thought to carry political messages, and their circulation was therefore tightly controlled and severely restricted by the state. Imported Western films are still tightly controlled in today's China: only thirty foreign titles are allowed to be shown annually, which compete with roughly thirty films that are produced and released domestically each month. All imported films have to be approved for how they depict political events and Chinese history, as well as their erotic content. In India, restrictions on distribution have often been motivated by cultural values: movies continue to be selected and banned for their sexually explicit scenes, nudity or plots that break the acceptable norms of conduct.

Against the popular perception of digital media flowing freely, there exists the reality of stoppages and bottlenecks and of complex landscapes of differentiated access. The share of waiting for an anticipated product is unevenly distributed around the world: 'the wait grows longer as you move from the northern hemisphere toward the Global South, and from metropolises to small towns and villages' (Liang and Sundaram 2011, 350). This evokes images of 'centre' and 'periphery' not as the established sociopolitical hierarchies that define cultural tastes and aesthetics, but as two modes of cultural consumption, one defined as 'licit' and another 'illicit', or pirate. If coming into contact with the 'culture of the other' – a space of critical distance 'from which she can contemplate and engage with difference' (Ossman 2013, 23) – through consumption indeed provides foundations for being 'worldly', then the options available to the cosmopolitan to take a particular route bear an enormous impact on her resulting cosmopolitanism. In the next session I examine this relationship in closer detail.

Cosmopolitanism of the abject

Consumption of culture today, with its concomitant disassociation with identities and publics from territories, publics and cultures, takes place in the context of this uneven access, whether it is due to lags in technology, state politics or business culture. As a result, there is an urgent need to rethink 'the possibilities of cultural engagement, social affiliations, legal authority and political action' (Nyers 2003, 1072) reflected in illegal – 'pirate' – media economies contrary to those afforded by licit markets. In this and the following sections I utilize the notion of 'abject cosmopolitanism' as a tool to, first, reveal the cosmopolitan nature of aspirations labeled as 'piracy' and, second, to rethink the industry's linking of global citizenry with copyright.

So far I have argued that the globalization of culture in late modernity created the uneven set of dynamics and processes, making it clear that practices of engaging with transnational culture have also been radically variegated. Unequal access, whether due to lagging in technology, state politics or business culture, is the situational context in which the disassociation of identities and collectivities from territories, polities and cultures accompanies cultural consumption. This raises questions about 'the possibilities of cultural engagement, social affiliations, legal authority and political action beyond the state' (Nyers 2003, 1072) accommodated by illegal media economies.

Although there is an intimate relationship between modernity and the cosmopolitan ideal (Beck and Grande 2010; Breckenridge et al. 2002; Calhoun 2007; Cheah 1998; Harvey 2009), the sophisticated demeanour of the worldly modern can be imagined differently in different contexts. In India, where technology chronically malfunctions, participation in a pirate economy is driven by the aspiration 'to inhabit the space of global time represented by and through the movies, where things are not perpetually breaking down' (Liang and Sundaram 2011). In Algeria, the pirate access to the image of foreign lands is not only sought for the entertainment it provides, but is also 'a means of "getting away" from a daily life made of economic difficulties and democratic insufficiencies' (Labandji quoted in Mattelart 2012, 738). Assembling a piece of music through a bit-torrent and maintaining relationships with illegal distributors is essential to many Russians' self-images as culturally savvy and well informed (Sezneva 2012). In these examples, listening to certain music, viewing a particular film and wearing a specific brand of clothing allows individuals to mimic a kind of modern subject who is not otherwise attainable either through national political institutions or domestic economic development (Thomas 2012). In this sense, Brian Larkin (2008, 226) argues, piracy is not antithetical to modernity but is its salient structure.

The irony, however, is that in contrast to the subjects of the wealthy core, for whom being 'modern' does not necessarily represent a tension with their national or localistic attachments, the subject of the periphery must leave behind the local and adopt the cosmopolitan stance to attain modernity for themselves: they inhabit, however imaginatively, the times and spaces that are not always their own. To paraphrase David Harvey (2000), such inhabitation represents a contrast between the purported universality and ethics of cosmopolitanism and the intractable particularities of the world geography. In this context, piracy is a specific vehicle of the cosmopolitan imagination – its vernacular expressions in every-day life. It is the only means with which people gain access to that cosmopolitan space.

If the previous examples situate piracy in the context of aspiring for modernity that is not based on identifying with a particular polity or sociality (Russian viewers enjoying *Dallas* do not become more Amer-ican), the case of fandoms reveals how piracy is instrumental in community building that is worldwide. Fans of the film trilogy *The Lord of the Rings* may reside in close to 100 different countries, and the readership of the novel span nearly forty languages. Individually and together they share extensive and detailed knowledge of their object. They are heavily emotionally connected to it and they spend large amounts of time exchanging their experiences with other like-minded people (Kloet and Zoonen 2007, 323). 'Piracy', however, is common among them (Pang 2012) whether they inhabit the economically developed core or the periphery.

Take American fans of Japanese anime: living in one of the most technologically advanced economies, they still had to resort to illegal copying and translation in the early 2000s, travelling to Japan to physically record anime episodes onto tapes. This was because the gold standard, where television episodes are available for viewing as soon as they air in Japan in the context of the standard distribution structure in the USA, was unattainable: the waiting time between an episode's release and its availability via legitimate channels generally ranged from several months to several years (Koulikov 2010, 3.1). Broadband internet changed this situation significantly – the waiting time shrank, communities expanded, while ties within them weakened – but the practice of illegal downloading and fan dubbing continues.

In China, lovers of Western movies, particularly art house, self-identified as 'D-buffs', where 'D' stood for both 'disc' and 'piracy'. Access ranked and assigned different prestige: those who purchased whatever was available on the pirate market – the basic level was called 'silly kids', – stood much lower on the pecking order than the avid and skilled in 'disc laundering'. They went after the best illegal copy and were ranked level five and called 'deity' (Li 2012, 547). This fan community shared some characteristics with the American anime fans in the emotional appeal that illegality itself possessed, tied to the thrill of the catch, the transgression and the exception to the rule of the majority.

The impact of illegal distribution in China, however, extended beyond mere self-styling. Grounding her argumentation in the work of media scholar Miriam Hansen, Li contends that the viral infrastructure of piracy in China has shaped an alternative public sphere – the 'non-disciplined' and 'shadow spectator community'. Hansen herself sought to address the apparent contradiction of cinema's spectatorship going private, while the articulation of experience remained collective and political. Redressing the definition of 'public' in terms of a 'social horizon of experience', Hansen saw this shift as 'a mixture of competing modes of organizing experience', thus redefining 'public' not in terms of co-presence – the (public) act of screening – but as a set of relations between the film and its audience.[2] This is an important distinction. In the context of a reformed China, this meant that that publicity based on co-presence invites control, while publicity based on a shared desire and experience of a cinematic text escapes the confinement of the official order, or 'policing'. 'Film consumption through piracy fashions a much less organized film spectatorship' (Li 2012, 558). This places piracy in the centre of a critical practice aimed at the political machinations of the state, notorious for inspiring nationalistic sentiment in its citizens.

The examples provided in this section illustrate the plurality of cosmopolitan stances, ranging from the subjectivity of the modern to the post-colony to the critical citizen of post-communism to the passionate connoisseur of an obscure aesthetics in the Western core. These different politics are facilitated to a varying degree by illegal distribution. However, for most transnational audiences, as Li notes, the political potential of such practice remains hidden. In the next section I consider some of the reasons for why this might be the case.

IPR as a police order

The historian of piracy Adrian Johns (2009) provocatively stated that any of us, as contemporary consumers, may at some point or another, fall under the category of 'pirate'. Toby Miller's use of the word 'trickster' at the opening of this paper captures the same unstable nature of the category. Miller's observation about pirates who 'liberate text from its owners'[3] is echoed in the work of Alex Dent, who poignantly argues that the derogation of piracy is inseparable from the neo-liberal fundamentalism of property, ownership and their exclusivity. The process of derogation of the 'pirate' resembles that of abjection of the 'asylum seeker': 'the abject-subject has an important constitutive role in self/other encounter' (Nyers 2003, 1072; Dent 2012, 31). The mutual constitution of piracy and the neo-liberal regime of commodity circulation bring us back to Rancière's notion of 'policing' and the task of examining how the 'cosmos' of copyright has been constructed.

For something that gets so much attention, it may first seem surprising that legal definitions of piracy are scarce, non-transparent and subject to constant revision. In 2005, UNESCO published a report that radically departed from an earlier and widely accepted definition of 'piracy' as 'acts intentionally committed with the goal of obtaining a commercial advantage of some kind' to 'significant damage to the interests of those right holders whose protection is the aim of intellectual property regimes' and indicated that 'this damage is increasingly sustained by conduct with little or no commercial motivation' (Mattelart 2009, 310). One of the advisers of the report was Darrell Panetherie, formerly vice president for legal and business affairs for Warner Brothers Music (1999–2004) and a principal litigator in high-profile cases such as Napster, mp3.com and Kazaa.

Collapsing the distinction between counterfeiting and piracy and linking piracy to organized crime has been another common strategy. The Agreement on Trade-Related Aspects of Intellectual Property Rights (TRIPS Agreement) Article 51, which provided the primary framework on international copyright and enforcement, clearly distinguishes between trademark infringement ('counterfeit') and copyright infringement ('piracy'). This distinction informed two different enforcement regimes. However, there is an ongoing conflation of these two terms by copyright enforcement agencies. Toys, medicine, food and international fashion brands are increasingly included in public discussions of substandard goods, as are illegally copied or downloaded music and movies. The conflation ties copyright infringement to a wide range of public safety issues and health risks, turning the distribution and consumption of cultural products that are produced without a licence into the 'dark side' of globalization.

Although copyright infringement was not initially viewed as a variant of organized crime, recent research financed and supported by industries has increasingly linked the two. A 2009 report produced by RAND Corporation presented fourteen case studies that allegedly demonstrated the involvement of media pirates in organized crime, including trafficking drugs and weapons, and three case studies that illustrated financial linkages to 'terrorist groups'. It proposed, among other things, that 'pirates' contribute to financing 'Islamic terrorist organizations, such as Hezbollah', threatening not merely the economic stability of certain corporations but the national security of a number of states (Treverton 2009, xi–xii, 6, 75–82). While the evidentiary basis is thin (Karaganis et al. 2011), the report scored high by connecting copyright infringement to 'crimes that the public are really scared of' (Drahos and Braithwaite 2002, 27).

The new order does not rest on expert knowledge alone. Public spectacles of the violent destruction of illicit discs and tapes and well-known celebrities addressing the public constitute the stock of public education by anti-piracy activism. In Russia in the 1990s, pirated discs were amassed in the Red Square and crushed by streamrollers. The event was nationally televised. In India, a similar spectacle took place but this time the discs were trampled by elephants. In Brazil, since 2005, 3 December has become the designated National Day of Combatting Piracy and Biopiracy, and discs are publicly destroyed with sledgehammers. Dent (2012, 33) vividly describes a Brazilian advertising campaign representative of what he calls 'a kind of semantic warfare'. This policing has its own transnational side: because public awareness is an area where coordination among industry groups is relatively easy, local campaigns tend to look alike from one country to the next. Here again, the transnationalization of production (of the campaigns) supports the naturalization of 'intellectual property' globally, thus transposing copyright to the status of the universal 'rule of law'. Crucially, this universality requires not only a shift in the legal field or a new institutional monitoring of activities, but also the emergence of a subject whose 'cosmos' includes an ideological belief in the dependency of creativity on exclusive ownership that transcends a specific time and place.

From policing to politicizing: conclusion

My focus on the expansion of IPRs regulating the global circulation of music and movies highlights the connection between the transnationalization of cultural production on the one hand, and the promotion of the particular ethical stance towards the rights of ownership, on the other. Intellectual property enforcement operates by activating a specific social imaginary in which creators, producers and their audiences are reciprocally bounded and form a common semantic universe. It positions this particular form of boundedness as normative and universal. Piracy, in this context, emerges as a countermovement that threatens to destroy this universe, and is increasingly constituted by anti-piracy activism as 'abject'.

One goal in my paper was to examine what socio-technological conditions lie behind this countermovement; another was to consider the forms of consciousness that the countermovement consequently supports. I argue that the prevailing effect of legal distribution – especially in the so-called developing world – is to restrict access, not universalize it, effectively provincializing many audiences and their identities, not transnationalizing them. Contrary to what anti-piracy advocates argue, piracy appears to be the grounded manifestation of the contradiction between aspiration and access, the economy of anticipation and the economy of distribution. When respected, IPRs restrict circulation to certain regions and marginalize the rest. They are an obstacle in the way of satisfying the desire to become worldly among the people that they regulate. From Brazil to Mali to Russia, piracy is a specific vehicle of the cosmopolitan imagination – its vernacular expression in everyday life. It is shot through and through with moral and political ambivalence related to economic development and collective self-perceptions vis-à-vis global inequalities.

Industries construe and represent piracy as a failure to participate in the ethical universe of the 'enlightened' cosmopolitan consumer defined by the sanctity of privacy of intellectual property. To echo Dent (2012), piracy politically constructed stands in contrast to the purity of legal consumption, to the authoritative, visible and politically modern subject. The representation itself, however, is not accidental, but operates by obfuscating other logics of, and alternative paths to, becoming a 'citizen of the world'. IPR represents the 'police order' in the sense formulated by Rancière, as it defines what is visible and legible, sayable and not, legitimate and illicit. It is in this sense that the 'cosmopolitan vision' mediated by copyright laws 'polices', while piracy, in contrast, 'politicizes'. By bringing together different strands of the literature on piracy, this paper has intended to better elucidate the discrepancies between the realities of cosmopolitan self-fashioning afforded by semiotic capacities of culture in circulation and the imperatives of economic value preservation accommodated by the would-be universal sanctity of copyright.

Notes

1. I chose to focus on this basic and in some sense primary definition of 'cosmopolitanism', although the debate in the literature has evolved to include much more: a cultural critique based on the unexpected absorption of ostensible difference, the cutting edge and so forth (see Dent 2009; Erlmann 1994; Straw 1991).
2. One may also relate here to Michael Warner (2002) and how he addresses two different registers of world-making: the public and the political. The key to Warner's thinking is the definition of a public as a group rhetorically hailed by strangers – 'Hey, you!' or 'my fellow Americans'. It is this relation to the message that proscribes the expressive and behavioural possibilities of interaction. Warner's goal is thus not to explain the origin of a public, but to refocus the inquiry on reflexive behaviour and the imaginative projections that characterize different kinds of publics.
3. See the opening quote of the paper.

References

Aronczyk, Melissa, and Ailsa Craig. 2012. "Introduction: Cultures of Circulation." *Poetics* 40 (2): 93–100. doi:10.1016/j.poetic.2012.02.001.

Beck, Ulrich, and Edgar Grande. 2010. "Varieties of Second Modernity: The Cosmopolitan Turn in Social and Political Theory and Research." *British Journal of Sociology* 61 (3): 409–443.

Beck, Ulrich, and Natan Sznaider. 2010. "Unpacking Cosmopolitanism for the Social Sciences: A Research Agenda." *The British Journal of Sociology* 61 (January): 381–403. doi:10.1111/j.1468-4446.2009.01250.x.

Breckenridge, Carol A., Sheldon Pollock, Homi K. Bhabha, and Dipesh Chakrabarty, eds. 2002. *Cosmopolitanism*. Durham, NC: Duke University Press Books.

Brennan, Timothy. 1997. *At Home in the World: Cosmopolitanism Now.* Cambridge, MA: Harvard University Press.

Calhoun, Craig J. 2007. *Nations Matter: Culture, History, and the Cosmopolitan Dream.* London and New York: Routledge

Calhoun, Craig. 2010. "Cosmopolitan Liberalism and Its Limits." In *Cosmopolitanism*, edited by R. Robertson. New York, NY: Sage.

Chambers, Ian. 1992. "Traveling Sounds: Whose Center, Whose Periphery?" *Popular Music Perspectives* 3: 141–146.

Cheah, Pheng. 1998. "Introduction Part II: The Cosmopolitical – Today." In *Cosmopolitics: Thinking and Feeling Beyond the Nation*, 20–43. Minneapolis: University of Minnesota Press.

Cheah, Pheng, Bruce Robbins, and Social Text Collective. 1998. *Cosmopolitics: Thinking and Feeling beyond the Nation.* Minneapolis: University of Minnesota Press.

Dent, Alexander. 2009. *River of Tears: Country Music, Memory, and Modernity in Brazil.* Durham, NC: Duke University Press.

Dent, Alexander. 2012. "Introduction: Understanding the War on Piracy, Or Why We Need More Anthropology of Pirates." *Anthropological Quarterly* 85 (3): 659–672.

Drahos, Peter, and John Braithwaite. 2002. *Information Feudalism: Who Owns the Knowledge Economy?* London: Earthscan.

Erlmann, Veit. 1994. "'Africa Civilised, Africa Uncivilized': Local Culture, World System and South African Music'." *Journal of Southern African Studies* 20 (2): 165–179. doi:10.1080/03057079408708394.

Erlmann, Veit. 1996. "The Aesthetics of the Global Imagination: Reflections on World Music in the 1990s." *Public Culture* 8: 476–487. doi:10.1215/08992363-8-3-467.

Fiske, John. 1992. "Cultural Studies and the Culture of Everyday Life." In *Cultural Studies*, edited by Lawrence Grossberg, Cary Nelson, and Paula Treichler, 154–173. New York: Routledge.

Gaonkar, Dilip Parameshwar, and Elizabeth A. Povinelli. 2003. "Technologies of Public Forms: Circulation, Transfiguration, Recognition." *Public Culture* 15 (3): 385–397. doi:10.1215/08992363-15-3-385.

Goldsmith, Ben, Susan Ward, and Tom O'Regan. 2012. "Global and Local Hollywood." *InMedia. The French Journal of Media and Media Representations in the English-Speaking World*, no. 1 (March). Accessed January 30 2014. http://inmedia.revues.org/114.

Guilbault, Jocelyne. 2001. "World Music." In *The Cambridge Companion to Pop and Rock*, edited by Simon Frith, Will Straw, and John Street, 176–193. Cambridge: Cambridge University Press.

Hansen, Miriam. 1994. *Babel and Babylon: Spectatorship in American Silent Film.* Cambridge, MA: Harvard University Press.

Harvey, David. 2000. "Cosmopolitanism and the Banality of Geographical Evils." *Public Culture* 12 (2): 529–564. doi:10.1215/08992363-12-2-529.

Harvey, David. 2009. *Cosmopolitanism and the Geographies of Freedom.* 1st ed. New York, NY: Columbia University Press.

Hiskey, Daven. 2013. "What Does Gangnam Style Mean?" *Today I Found Out.* Accessed December 30. http://www.todayifoundout.com/index.php/2012/12/what-does-gangnam-style-mean/.

Johns, Adrian. 2009. *Piracy: The Intellectual Property Wars from Gutenberg to Gates*. Chicago, IL: University of Chicago Press.

Karaganis, Joe. 2011. "Chapter 1: Re-thinking Piracy." In *Media Piracy in Emerging Economies*, edited by Joe Karaganis, 1–74. New York: SSRC Books.

Karaganis, Joe, Pedro Mizukami, Lawrence Liang, John Cross, and Olga Sezneva. 2011. "Does Crime Pay? MPEE's Findings on Piracy, Organized Crime, Nad Terrorism." Findings. SSRC. Accessed February 1 2014. http://piracy.american-assembly.org/wp-content/uploads/2011/02/Does-Crime-Pay.pdf.

Karaganis, Joe, and Lennart Renkema. 2013. *Copy Culture in the US and Germany*. New York: The American Assembly & Columbia University. Accessed January 30 2014. http://americanassembly.org/sites/americanassembly.org/files/download/project/copy-culture.pdf.

Kiriya, Ilya. 2012. "The Culture of Subversion and Russian Media Landscape." *International Journal of Communication* 6: 446–466.

Kloet, Jeroen de, and Lisbeth van Zoonen. 2007. "Fan Culture." In *Media Studies: Key Issues and Debates*, edited by Eoin Devereux, 320–334. New York, NY: Sage.

Koulikov, Mikhail. 2010. "Fighting the Fan Sub War: Conflicts between Media Rights Holders and Unauthorized Creator/distributor Networks." *Transformative Works and Cultures* 5. Accessed January 29 2014. http://journal.transformativeworks.org/index.php/twc/article/view/115/171.

Kuipers, G., and J. de Kloet. 2009. "Banal Cosmopolitanism and the Lord of the Rings: The Limited Role of National Differences in Global Media Consumption." *Poetics* 37 (2): 99–118. doi:10.1016/j.poetic.2009.01.002.

Larkin, Brian. 2008. *Signal and Noise: Media, Infrastructure, and Urban Culture in Nigeria*. Durham, NC: Duke University Press.

Latour, Bruno. 2013. "Whose Cosmos, Which Cosmopolitics? Comments on the Peace Terms of Ulrich Beck." *Common Knowledge* 10 (3): 450–462.

Li, Jinying. 2012. "Piracy Cultures| from 'D-Buffs' to the 'D-Generation': Piracy, Cinema, and an Alternative Public Sphere in Urban China." *International Journal of Communication* 6: 542–563.

Liang, Laurence, and Ravi Sundaram. 2011. "Chapter 8: India." In *Media Piracy in Emerging Economies*, edited by Joes Karaganis, 339–398. New York: SSRC Books.

Mattelart, Tristan. 1994. "Pre-1989 East-West Video – Entertainment without Borders." *Réseaux. The French Journal of Communication* 2 (2): 267–280. doi:10.3406/reso.1994.3282.

Mattelart, Tristan. 2009. "Audio-visual Piracy: Towards a Study of the Underground Networks of Cultural Globalization." *Global Media and Communication* 5 (3): 308–326.

Mattelart, Tristan. 2012. "Audiovisual Piracy, Informal Economy, and Cultural Globalization." *International Journal of Communication* 6: 735–750.

Miller, Toby. 2007. "Global Hollywood 2010." *International Journal of Communication* 1: 1–4.

Nyers, Peter. 2003. "Abject Cosmopolitanism: The Politics of Protection in the Anti-Deportation Movement." *Third World Quarterly* 24 (6): 1069–1093. doi:10.1080/01436590310001630071.

Ossman, Susan. 2013. *Moving Matters Paths of Serial Migration*. Standford, CA: Standford University Press.

Pang, Laikwan. 2012. *Creativity and Its Discontents: China's Creative Industries and Intellectual Property Rights Offenses*. Durham, NC: Duke University Press.

Rancière, Jacques. 2001. "Ten Theses on Politics." *Theory and Event* 5 (3): 1–11.

Rancière, Jacques. 2007. "What Does It Mean to Be Un?" *Continuum: Journal of Media and Cultural Studies* 21 (4): 559–569. doi:10.1080/10304310701629961.

Regev, Motti. 2013. *Pop-rock Music: Aesthetic Cosmopolitanism in Late Modernity*. Hoboken, NJ: John Wiley & Sons.

Saito, Hiro. 2011. "An Actor-Network Theory of Cosmopolitanism*." *Sociological Theory* 29 (2): 124–149. doi:10.1111/j.1467-9558.2011.01390.x.

Sezneva, Olga. 2012. "The Pirates of Nevskii Prospekt: Intellectual Property, Piracy and Institutional Diffusion in Russia." *Poetics* 40 (2): 150–166. doi:10.1016/j.poetic.2012.02.005.

Sezneva, Olga, and Sebastien Chavin. 2014. "Has Capitalism Gone Virtual? Value, Intellect and the Obscolescence of Commodity." *Critical Historical Studies* 1, 125–150. doi:10.1086/675381.

Stanley, Bob. 2012. "Sixty Years of the UK Charts." *The Guardian*, November 13. Accessed January 30 2014. http://www.guardian.co.uk/music/2012/nov/13/sixty-years-uk-charts.

Straw, Will. 1991. "Systems of Articulation, Logics of Change: Communities and Scenes in Popular Music." *Cultural Studies* 5 (3): 368–388. doi:10.1080/09502389100490311.

Sundaram, Ravi. 2009. *Pirate Modernity: Delhi's Media Urbanism*. 1st ed. London: T & F Books UK.

Thomas, Kedron. 2012. "Intellectual Property Law and the Ethics of Imitation in Guatemala." *Anthropological Quarterly* 85 (3): 785–815. doi:10.1353/anq.2012.0052.

Treverton, Gregory. 2009. *Film Piracy, Organized Crime and Terrorism*. RAND Corporation Monograph Series.

Warner, Michael. 2002. *Publics and Counterpublics*. New York: Zone Books and MIT Press.

Between global citizenship and Qatarization: negotiating Qatar's new knowledge economy within American branch campuses

Neha Vora

Over the last decade, the Gulf state of Qatar has invested billions of dollars in American branch campuses as part of its development as a 'knowledge-based economy'. A knowledge economy will allow Qatar to diversify from petroleum wealth and reduce the country's reliance on foreign labour by introducing more citizens into the workforce, a process called 'Qatarization'. While intended to bolster nativism, branch campuses are organized around certain Western liberal norms, such as meritocracy, egalitarianism and multiculturalism. These manifest in several ways, including English education, gender integration and a student body that is composed of more non-citizens than Qatari nationals. In this article, I explore how non-citizen students in particular, many of who were born and raised in Qatar, interact with Qatar's new knowledge economy, paying particular attention to the seemingly contradictory models of 'global citizenship' on the one hand and 'Qatarization' on the other – one a philosophy that is open and inclusive, and the other specifically closed and exclusive.

Situated on the outskirts of Doha, Qatar's capital, Education City houses branch campuses of six top American universities: Northwestern, Georgetown, Cornell, Carnegie Mellon, Texas A&M and Virginia Commonwealth. The sprawling compound, which continues to grow and add new educational offerings, is a multi-billion dollar investment by the government of Qatar – overseen by a body called the Qatar Foundation – intended to grow the country's 'knowledge economy' in order to diversify away from its finite petroleum wealth (Krieger 2008).[1] The state's hope is that an indigenous knowledge economy will in turn produce more skilled

Qatari citizens for the workforce, thereby also reducing the country's heavy reliance on foreign workers, who currently constitute over 85% of the population. This practice, called 'Qatarization', is official state policy and is actively promoted in several ways: companies are offered incentives to incorporate more Qataris and Qataris receive preferential treatment in many educational and hiring processes. Qatar's American universities, therefore, are an investment in a knowledge economy that primarily fosters nativist national identity and Qatarization. However, because they are imagined and administered as extensions of their home campuses in the USA, Education City's American universities are underpinned by Western liberal ideologies – namely multiculturalism, egalitarianism, secularism, democracy and liberal feminism – that do not always match up with Qatari understandings of national futures and traditional values. These ideologies manifest in several key ways, including gender-integrated classrooms, English-only education, curricula that foster critical thinking on topics like religion and sexuality, student government, and a large population of non-citizen students and employees. In fact, there are only a handful of Qataris in the faculty and higher administration of Education City institutions, and non-Qataris – mostly South Asian and Arab young people who were born and raised in Doha – comprise more than 50% of the student body at most schools. This demographic make-up mirrors that of the country, but is also the result of a bifurcated primary and secondary (K-12) education system: public schooling for Qataris in Arabic (and more recently in English) is not as competitive or as preparatory for American-style higher education as the mainly English-medium private school options that serve the country's large foreign resident and elite citizen population. These private schools also provide citizenship training that prepares young people for the possibility for cosmopolitan existences in other parts of the world, because it is expected that they will attend university in their 'home' countries or in the West. Thus, while Qatar is one of the world's most 'international' countries, most foreign residents grow up relatively segregated by nationality and with little sustained contact with Qataris, especially within school contexts.[2]

Because the Qatari government has designed Education City to provide 'American' education, recruited primarily Americans to fill key positions, and looked to the USA as a source of expertise for the growth of an indigenous knowledge economy, the project has heightened local concerns about too much Western influence, which might result in the loss of Arabic language, Muslim values and traditional Qatari social relations. Education City has also raised questions among Qataris about who is benefitting more from its universities: citizens or migrants? All of these tensions and debates about higher education in Qatar seem to revolve around a critical paradox embedded within Education City itself: that it is through liberal (and neo-liberal) education that non-liberal aspirations of national futures can be achieved.

In this article, I explore how students in Education City – particularly non-citizens – navigate what appears to be a disjunction between Qatarization, a policy that structurally favours citizens, and an American-style university system that is charged with actively promoting a form of cosmopolitan 'global citizenship' based on a belief in individualism, meritocracy and multiculturalism. While Qatari citizens receive great welfare benefits from the petro-state, foreign residents are tied to temporary renewable work visas or are dependents of those on work visas in a migrant sponsorship system called *kafala* – neither they nor their children have access to citizenship or even permanent residency, regardless of the number of years, or even generations, they have resided and worked in the Gulf (Ali 2010; Gardner 2010; Leonard 2003; Vora 2009, 2013). The structural inequalities bred by the *kafala* system and by Qatarization permeated into the daily lives of college students, even as they negotiated new forms of identity and citizenship that were enabled by liberal and neo-liberal educational models. While these contradictory models seem to have been born of institutional migration to a non-liberal context like Doha, I explore in this article how Qatari non-liberal state policies and American liberal higher education are actually not as incommensurable as they seem. The astute critiques and insights by actors engaged with American branch campuses that I present here – particularly those of foreign resident students – in fact reveal various ways in which non-American students often experienced and perceived American higher education in the USA as more exclusionary than they did their educational experience in Qatar, despite the inbuilt forms of structural inequality that they faced within Education City as non-citizens; thus, contrary to the American academy's discourse of being based in ideals of freedom and democracy, it may in fact be more inviting to students in its seemingly unequal and non-meritocratic Qatari incarnation than it would be to them in the USA. In addition, the impacts of global neo-liberal trends make partnerships between American universities and non-democratic contexts like the Gulf States quite mutually beneficial (Olds and Thrift 2005; Ong 2006).

The research findings presented here are based on over six months of preliminary ethnographic fieldwork conducted in Education City, Doha between 2010 and 2012, which included extensive participant observation in the social spaces of Education City universities; sixteen formal interviews and dozens of daily conversations with faculty, students and administrators at these schools; and three summer sessions of teaching introductory anthropology at Texas A& M Qatar (TAMUQ).[3] This project, which is still in its early stages, develops out of – and builds on – insights from my previous fieldwork in Dubai, where I encountered several South Asian young people who had attended or were attending new American-style universities that were beginning to proliferate in the Gulf (Vora 2013). These young people, who often found themselves interacting with Gulf nationals for the first time in their lives at these campuses, articulated forms of citizenship and identity that differed from my other informants' narratives. This indicated a growing politicization around what many of these young people called their 'second-class citizenship' in the United Arab Emirates. I became interested in what impacts American institutions of higher education were having on Gulf societies, particularly on migrants and on women, who also were attending these schools in large numbers. I chose Qatar as my research site because of its large branch campus initiative, Education City. The ethnographic data I present here are part of a larger project in which I am exploring in greater detail the on-the-ground negotiations, challenges and experiences of transferring American educational models to a non-Western, non-liberal and non-democratic country like Qatar. This early account of what is happening on the ground provides some insights into the project of globalizing American higher education that go beyond the parochial top-down debates about the value and threat of branch campuses to American academe that are currently circulating in the USA as part of larger critiques of neo-liberal university restructuring.

American higher education in the Gulf: producing a local global university

Contemporary American higher education has been increasingly focused on the 'global' as a value-add to the forms of citizenship national education fosters, and as a strategy for competing for resources and student 'clients' in an increasingly neo-liberal arena, by which I mean the growing influence of market logics upon academia (Slaughter and Rhoades 2009). This 'global' orientation takes a number of forms, including recruitment of international students to home campuses; implementation of Global Studies, International Affairs, and other programmes that move away from Cold War era area-studies models; growth in study abroad opportunities for American students; and, most recently, expansion through partnerships or branch campuses into areas outside of the USA, particularly those with growing economies. Although a 'global' or cosmopolitan outlook is not new to the concept of Western academe in any way, and there have been Western academic enterprises in many parts of the world both during and after the colonial period, scholars have noted something 'new' about this current moment, especially pertaining to American branch campuses in places like the Gulf states (Miller-Idriss and Hanauer 2011). This newness is connected, according to a range of scholars and critics, to the increasingly neo-liberal and corporate nature of the American university, as well as to the specific challenges and concerns that profit-making ventures in non-liberal and non-democratic states pose to the values of academic freedom, critical thinking and disinterested knowledge production (see e.g. Aksan 2010; Altbach 2004b; Sidhu, Ho, and Yeoh 2011). Some claim that this new global American university is an extension of previous models, one in which American imperialism is just recast in a different form (see e.g. Altbach 2004a). In particular, the histories of American University in Beirut (AUB) and American University in Cairo (AUC), which both started as Christian missionary projects, could be considered as part of this longer history in the region, and as models for newer projects like Education City (Bertelsen 2012). Others, however, note a break from colonial modes of academe and argue instead that it is the corporate nature of the university, authoritarian regimes and the new 'empire' of dispersed capital that threaten the ideals of the Western academy (Morey 2004; Poovey 2001). There are in fact very few voices from academics themselves in support of such ventures, and most see them as administrative projects that exemplify negative changes in the university structure over the last few decades.[4]

In two relatively recent articles, Lim (2009) and Looser (2012) ask specifically about the forms of global citizenship that branch campuses might be producing. Looser, basing his work partly on NYU Abu Dhabi, argues that contemporary global citizenship is less connected to the local, and thus more problematic than the forms fostered by earlier area-studies models. Lim, on the other hand, draws connections with previous forms of colonial institutions of learning in the Global South, arguing that what used to be an 'outpost complex' has been replaced with an 'edifice complex' – the need to expand the university in ways that make it appear at once more 'global' and more 'world class'. However, in the process, Lim argues, only certain disciplinary formations travel across borders, (re)producing a binary in which the academic metropole produces scholars while branch campuses focus on vocational training. Thus, the 'global' training that students in branch campuses receive is less nuanced than what is available at home campuses and is linked primarily to neo-liberal outcomes of self-making and economic success upon graduation.[5]

Both Lim and Looser build upon the idea that a new formation of empire, one that is based in capital, manifests itself within the global university. While the forms that the 'global' take in the contemporary world are indeed infused with neo-liberal logics, the global and the neo-liberal as interchangeable and equivalent are taken for granted in much of the criticism of branch campuses in ways that I feel need to be unpacked and problematized. In addition, much writing on the branch campuses themselves and their specificities often favours an equation in which the model of the liberal/neo-liberal globalizing university (and its ideologies) takes precedence over the various ways that it gets entangled with local ideas about education, futures, prestige and citizenship, and is experienced by diverse students, faculty and staff.[6]

While there has been great debate within American academia about what branch campuses represent for the future of liberal education, there is very little existing ethnographic research about the way that the branch campus is generated and lived on the ground. What research does exist is limited to short-term or exploratory work (Kelly 2010; Tetrault 2010; Vora 2013, forthcoming). As the anthropology of education has long argued, schools are not merely sites of top-down social reproduction, but also spaces in which differently situated actors produce new meanings and identifications as they interact with ideological forms, curricula and each other (Collins 2009; Yon 2003). In particular, anthropologists have explored how race, gender, religion, language and immigration status are key factors that impact how students craft identity, belonging and citizenship, often within conditions of marginalization (Lukose 2007; Sarroub 2005). Many educational historians, theorists and anthropologists have argued therefore that Western higher education is just as foundationally hierarchical and exclusive as it is interested in promoting democracy and inclusivity (Althusser 2006; Apple 2004; Levinson, Foley, and Holland 1996; Rosaldo 1994).

My project is interested in both the inclusive/democratic and exclusive/ hierarchical underpinnings of the American academy, and how these have shifted alongside globalization and a mounting interest in producing global citizenship among students. Elitism and exclusion are structurally part of the American academy in its original instantiation – and today we continue to experience them in our marked bodily movements through the spaces of academe, through the shifting structure of academic labour and in the ways that our work is legible or illegible to certain audiences. However, particular nostalgic mythologies of the university as an idealized space circulate in academic lamentations of the 'new' corporate globalized higher education form, particularly in the critiques that faculty have made of branch campuses and other partnership ventures with non-liberal states. I am interested in exploring what is elided in these critiques, and how my work can interrupt or intervene in some of the stories that we tell ourselves about academe's past, present and future, even as we are deeply impacted by our own inequalities and changes in our own institutional and disciplinary spaces. Therefore, instead of asking whether Western educational values are eroding through globalization and branch campus expansion, I explore the ways that institutions and their values are transformed when they enter into new contexts, the entanglements of different ideologies and visions that occur in the making of branch campuses, and new forms of citizenship and identity that are produced within these spaces of higher education.

Diversity and hierarchy within a two-tier system

In August 2011, I was finishing up a summer of research in Education City, which also included a short stint as a visiting assistant professor at TAMUQ, a position I had held the previous year and would be invited to fill again. My interviewee that day was a young Indian man, Aman, who had just graduated and was about to start a master's programme in engineering in the USA. Although it was the middle of Ramadan, several students had heard from their peers about my interest in their college experiences and were eager to speak with me; Aman had actually contacted me to set up an interview, despite it taking place in the middle of the day when most of the Muslim population of the city was resting. Like many non-Qatari students in Education City, Aman was born and raised in Qatar. However, despite growing up in a diverse international city like Doha, he had attended an Indian-only K-12 system that was gender-segregated. For Aman, entering TAMUQ was a challenge because he had to learn to interact regularly both with women and with other nationalities, including Qataris, for the first time in his life. In addition, as a foreign resident, and unlike his Qatari counterparts, he was not able to readily access company sponsorships that would pay his way through college and guarantee him employment after graduation.

While Qatari citizens receive great welfare benefits from the petro-state, foreign residents have few rights and privileges, and are subject to differential governance, fear of deportation and discrimination in many realms of their life. This 'second-class citizenship', as many of my young interlocutors in Dubai had described it – which is not formally citizenship at all – extends into the structure of higher education in Qatar and the Gulf states, particularly Education City, which offers a unique opportunity for expatriates to enrol in university in the Gulf instead of having to return to home countries or enter Western institutions, as they did in the past (Vora 2013, forthcoming). But while the American university is based on ideas of meritocracy and egalitarianism, the state policy of Qatarization, along with the kafala system, affects the opportunities available to students based on their nationality. In particular, the financial burdens of attending elite universities and the insecurities of obtaining employment upon graduation that expatriate students face are almost entirely absent for their Qatari counterparts.

Qatari students almost always enter university on some kind of sponsorship system. They are either recruited by companies in Qatar or get sponsorships from Qatar Foundation, the umbrella organization that oversees knowledge economy creation in Qatar. A sponsorship pays for their tuition and provides them with summer internships as well as a generous stipend. In return, they are required to give back time to their sponsoring company for the number of years that they were in school. This system keeps them tied to the Qatari economy, but also provides them with guaranteed employment and free education. Often their undergraduate stipends add up to thousands of dollars per month, making college life profitable for them and their families. On the other hand, foreign resident students (those who are dependents of family members employed in the Gulf Cooperation Council countries) have very little access to sponsorships. They are, however, able to apply for generous financial aid through Qatar Foundation in the form of an interest-free loan to be paid back after graduation, which is how Aman financed his education at TAMUQ. Many foreign residents also pay out of pocket, as do the small number of international students coming to Qatar to attend university or coming from US home campuses on short study-abroad trips.

Foreign residents are not guaranteed employment in Qatar after graduation and often find they have to compete for lesser positions among a larger pool of expatriates because Qatarization policies mean that nationals enjoy preferential hiring. Thus, non-citizens face financial challenges and uncertain futures within branch campuses that Qataris do not, effectively creating a two-tier system of education in a space where equality is stressed as a founding pedagogical and student experience principal. This two-tier system also spills over into other aspects of college socialization. It is evident in the way that students interact with each other or avoid each other in hallways and social spaces, within student clubs, or in other extracurricular venues. However, despite these structural inequalities, Education City also gives rise to new ways of thinking about similarity and difference among students – and forms of global citizenship and cosmopolitanism – that both exceed and challenge existing social hierarchies and the overwhelmingly negative views that circulate among US academics about bringing globalized higher education to the Gulf.

Regardless of the challenges that he faced as a non-citizen in Education City, Aman did not regret his decision to attend TAMUQ. In fact, he felt that he received a better education at TAMUQ than he would have on the main campus in College Station, Texas. He was astounded, for example, at the equipment and laboratory space the school provided and at the opportunities to travel to conferences and on study-abroad trips to the main campus, which he took full advantage of. These trips made him realize how much personal attention he got from faculty and how many more resources he had access to in Doha. In addition, he was able to stay at home with his family while in college, instead of having to go abroad and adjust to a new location. But most of all, Aman insisted that TAMUQ gave him a much better education than an Indian or an American university would have because of its incredible diversity:

> I was used to just talking to somebody who looked like me or was the same background. This whole opportunity has pushed me to get out of my comfort zone, to, you know, make friends, to just learn to talk to people from different backgrounds. You know they teach you what to say, the social dos and don'ts when you are in a multicultural or multinational environment. I guess there has been a lot of learning experience subconsciously… The next generation of people that comes out is gonna be way different than the one that exists right now. And I can see and I can tell you that. People who have that mindset, that I appreciate and respect you regardless of where you are from.

For Aman, then, going to TAMUQ afforded him more opportunities, allowed him to stay close to home, challenged his parochialism within a space he was somewhat comfortable in, and taught him how to interact with a wider range of people on a daily basis. Many students, Qatari and foreign resident, in our informal hallway conversations as well as in our interviews, similarly expressed that the Education City university experience positively challenged their stereotypes about other nationalities. While foreign residents, particularly South Asians, told me that they were surprised to get to know that Qataris were not snobby, lazy or rude, Qataris expressed a greater respect for their non-Gulf counterparts, who they otherwise only interacted with primarily as service personnel. Amna, a Qatari student at Carnegie Mellon, related an incident that changed her outlook on being Qatari, and also showcased how identities in Education City were developing relationally in classrooms and other spaces:

> Some Qataris treat the Indians like they are servants. This is not right. One time there was a fight in class. They were in a group, an Indian and a Qatari. The Qatari was telling the Indian what to do, do this, do that, and the Indian said, "I am not your servant, you should talk to me properly."

This incident made Amna more aware of how she might be treating her non-Qatari peers, and led her to go out of her way to make friends outside of her national group. She went from seeing Indians as 'servants' to seeing them as peers, just as many Indians went from seeing Qataris as lazy and pushy to seeing them as hard-working group members and potential friends. Of course, many of these interview answers may have been scripted based both on what students feel they can say and on what they expect the Western researcher wants to hear. And I myself experienced tensions and forms of self-segregation that challenged these narratives. However, these scripts were in many ways what the students themselves had come to believe about themselves as university students within Education City, and had also begun to model based on their university experiences inside and outside of the classroom, especially in relation to family members and those who did not attend these schools (see e.g. Kane 2012). Sara, for example, a Qatari who was entering her senior year at TAMUQ, told me that what she liked best about the American university platform was that it centred on 'structure, professionalism, and objectivity' – a phrasing that represented her internalization of a particular form of neo-liberal citizenship that she encountered within Education City. However, students' neo-liberal and global citizenship claims were also infused with certain reaffirmed parochial understandings of difference and gender- or nationality-based privilege, as I explore below.

'Working together': undoing stereotypes and reaffirming difference

Many of the mission statements for Qatar Foundation and for the universities in Education City highlight a 'global' experience as a main student outcome goal. In addition, state discourses about knowledge economy also emphasize Qatar's need to become more outwardly focused in order to be competitive and internationally recognized. This global emphasis, then, is one that both increases Qatar's international recognition as a developing, modern, innovative country while working to create a national citizenship that is simultaneously cosmopolitan. This idea of the 'global' carries with it certain American or Western parochialisms that are both recognized as such and that have also become cosmopolitan norms that parents and students expect – such as English-language teaching, secular classrooms, gender integration and liberal democratic ideas about tolerance of multiculturalism (Vora forthcoming). How global citizenship actually gets framed by Education City institutions, however, is through the neo-liberal vocational orientation of the branch campuses, where students, rather than being exposed to a more general liberal arts experience, are instead most often trained to enter into specific fields after graduation.

If we only looked at the models of global citizenship espoused by Education City schools, then, the argument that they represent a manifestation of a new empire of capital (as Lim, Looser and others suggest) might be justified; however, we also need to consider how various actors engage with these models, how they interact with existing local frameworks, and how they produce forms of belonging and citizenship that exceed or contradict their original intent. While most of the administrators, students and faculty that I spoke to were aware that global citizenship effectively meant being able to eventually 'work together' as neo-liberal subjects in multinational environments, the experience of being able to interact with people from different back-grounds, to learn about different social contexts, and to travel to home campuses in the USA and to other parts of the world gave rise to a sense of being global and an ethos of cosmopolitanism that went beyond students' ability to 'work together' and beyond neo-liberal logics of self-making. Therefore, despite Education City's focus on global citizenship as instrumental to the job market, students were also taking up many of the liberal values that the American academy connects with global citizenship. What is key, however, is that these were adapted in ways that reflected the particularities of Doha's international yet stratified context, as well as students' own engagements with the burgeoning knowledge economy based on gender, race, nationality and a variety of other factors. In particular, students found that the Education City experience challenged their pre-existing stereotypes about different groups, made them less parochial in their outlook, and also highlighted some of the disparities that underpinned the two-tier system of education that Qatar Foundation offered. In spite of this, the multicultural or global experiences that they had at Education City also ended up at times reaffirming and reassembling the very forms of difference that students had begun to dismantle.

My conversation with Maya, for example, a Doha-raised Indian who had just finished her freshman year at TAMUQ, highlights how meeting people from different nationalities changed her outlook on working together, challenged her stereotypes and taught her how to interact with difference more successfully:

> Working in any sort of a multicultural environment, everyone faces some sort of challenge. More often than not it is because a certain set of people think differently, are taught to think differently than you. For example, if you look from afar you would think that Arabs are lazy; they like to take their work at their own pace. But that is their style and if you are in a place where there are more Arabs then you have to adapt yourself to that style, to get the best out of it. You can't say, "Ok, work only according to my style." There was a project last semester where a lot of people had trouble working, they had a lot of conflicts. But if you just try to see the other person's perspective, people could get along.

Maya's takeaway point here was not that we should *not* treat people differently based on nationality; in fact, it was quite the opposite. She continued:

> Now if I am working with an Egyptian this is how I deal with them, and if I am working with a Lebanese this is how I deal with them, and if I'm working with a Qatari this is how I deal with them, because it's different. You work with different people differently.

In the narratives and passing comments of students, faculty and administrators, this tendency to reify national difference after noting how it got disassembled in the spaces of Education City was quite common. The multinational environment of Education City therefore provided new experiences that challenged pre-existing stereotypes, through organized activities by faculty and administration, or through social interaction, or even emerging out of conflicts and tensions between students, which were also fairly common. However, Education City's multicultural environment and its focus on a neo-liberal global citizenship aimed at 'working together' also reconfigured understandings of people that were still in many ways nationality-based; through the process of finding modes of engagement that transcended ethno-national difference, students began to recuperate and reassemble ethno-national stereotypes and parochialisms anew. In addition, the structural way in which nationality mattered reared its head at times when students were building up ideas about meritocracy, egalitarianism and 'working together' in ways that highlighted the non-liberal aspects of this supposedly liberal and neo-liberal space. Specific-ally, it was when students needed to find internships and jobs – in their junior and senior years – that their unequal positions in Qatar based on nationality became starker.

Qatarization and meritocracy: multiple logics of belonging in Education City and American academia

Administrators, faculty and foreign resident students all acknowledged the structural disadvantage to non-citizens because of Qatarization, but they simultaneously professed a deep belief that meritocracy underpinned their education system. Foreign resident students in particular acknowledged that this unfair but necessary recruiting system existed even as they told me about their belief that Education City was a primarily egalitarian space. That these ideas could coexist in one interviewee's narrative – sometimes even in the same sentence – might make little sense to a US educator; however, I found that these narratives, and especially the ways in which my interlocutors compared Education City to American academia, revealed the liberal, neo-liberal and non-liberal aspects of the student experience in Qatar as well as at home campuses in the USA, logics that might seem on the surface to be at odds with each other, but in effect rely on each other to produce citizenship training, pedagogies, ideas about difference, forms of belonging and, often, disparate futures for college graduates, both in the USA and in Qatar.

Aman's interview provides a good example of how students find ways to reconcile these conflicts between hierarchy and egalitarianism. Although he praised TAMUQ and Education City for challenging students' preconceived notions of other nationalities, Aman was still aware that he was in a two-tier education system, where jobs and sponsorships were preferentially given to Qataris, and where expatriates like himself would both have a harder time procuring employment and would never be able to officially belong even if they worked in Qatar for several decades. Global citizenship, while an ideal that he and his counterparts believed in, was therefore inextricable from the bifurcated system that *kafala* and Qatarization produced. To illustrate, Aman described two classmates – one a Qatari woman, one a Bangladeshi man. They both were hired at the same time at the national gas company:

> He was better in grades but couldn't get hired as an engineer because of their policy [Qatarization]. He is a tech and she is his boss now. I put myself in that place [the Bangladeshi's] and I wonder how I would feel. I would feel bad… but also be grateful for the opportunity.

Many of my interlocutors stressed that the preferential treatment that Qataris received in admissions, sponsorships and placement was necessary since Qataris did not have the competitive advantage that other expatriates had based on a lack of cosmopolitan 'international' K-12 schooling – and since it was 'their country' after all. Middle- and upper-class foreign residents overwhelmingly espoused neo-liberal understandings of their successes in the Gulf: their ability to succeed when their compatriots did not, their salary levels in comparison to those of other nationalities, and their advancement in their careers was attributed by expatriate faculty, administrators and students to self-entrepreneurship and market fundamentalism. For example, American educators often explained that they made more in the Gulf because it was more difficult to convince Americans to come there, and many people justified differential salaries based on nationality to home country costs of living (Vora 2008, 2013). Aman's neo-liberal understandings of work ethic and success therefore coexisted quite seamlessly with his acceptance of the non-liberal policies of Qatarization; with systems of white/Western privilege that were built into Qatar's knowledge economy (Vora forthcoming); with the knowledge that free speech in the Gulf was not fully possible; and with a discourse of respect for 'host' country customs and laws, including Islamic practice, modesty and forms of gender segregation.

These 'multiple logics of belonging', as I have called them elsewhere (Vora 2013), permeate the spaces of Education City and of Qatar in general, but they are not unique to the Gulf context. In fact, the comparisons that my interlocutors made with American academic spaces and the USA revealed an understanding of similar multiple and contradictory logics at work there as well. Understanding these contradictions in Qatar prompted students to criticize the American academy, which, in their view, failed to live up to its egalitarian promise. Thus, students understood that global citizenship, meritocracy and egalitarianism, as constituted in the USA, were inherently unequal and did not become less equal or more flawed when they moved to a non-liberal space like Qatar.

Aman, for example, told me that he understood that Education City was primarily for Qataris, and that he was mostly fine with that; but having lived in Doha all his life and seen his father do well there, he felt that there should be some kind of security for foreign residents like his family members. At this point in the interview, I felt it necessary to ask Aman how, given the built-in advantages to citizens, Qatari forms of American higher education could ever be commensurable to those at the home campuses, which seemingly treat students more equally. Aman actually disagreed quite strongly with my assessment of the difference between American home campuses and branch campuses: 'But they have a bias there [USA] based on your visa status, you know, if you are an international student. Good luck getting a job, good luck getting an internship. Here you see what you are getting into.' This sentiment was echoed in many of my interviews across Education City and within my classroom as well – that the US system was also inherently discriminatory towards certain groups, particularly international students (especially those who were read as Arab or Muslim), who paid higher tuition fees, had trouble with visas and were less likely to find employment upon graduation in the USA than they would in Qatar, especially since the one-on-one opportunities to network and meet people in a small place like Doha were much higher.

In addition to the inequality that international students felt they would face in America, many who had visited the home campuses of their institutions came back very disillusioned with the USA, particularly its coldness and its racism. Qataris and other Muslim students felt disrespected and out of place in the drinking and dating culture of home campuses; South Asian and Arab students noted discrimination at the airport, in college towns and even in classrooms; and all students had trouble making friends, navigating the larger scale of the main campus, and getting face time with faculty members. As one Egyptian student at Georgetown told me: 'Qatar is very warm, especially the university – one guy goes to the vending machine and he brings back seven Pepsi cans because there are seven of us. That kind of environment, it's so warm. That's not an American mentality.'

The students that I met articulated a global citizenship that emerged from their experiences in Education City, one that distinctly pushed against an American or Western form of being global in favour of localized understandings of both their opportunities and their limitations as situated actors in a global economy. This was not a view from nowhere or a non-grounded global citizenship at all – nor was it simply the product of a neo-liberal project to 'work together' – but very much a view from somewhere that was also cosmopolitan at the same time (as all cosmopolitanisms are).[7] Qatarization and global citizenship lingered here as constantly evolving concepts that were both in tension and worked in tandem to produce grounded cosmopolitan identities for various actors in Education City.

Conclusion

The Qatari American university can teach us much about the on-the-ground effects of globalized higher education in the Gulf, about the ideas and vocabularies that underpin the American academy's sense of itself and how these concepts are thought of as transportable, and about how liberal educational forms are policed as accessible or 'not yet' accessible to differently situated actors around the world (Chakrabarty 2000). While the conversations around globalized higher education occurring from within metropolitan 'home' campuses has largely centred on the ways in which expansion to non-liberal spaces like the Gulf Arab states, Singapore or China will dilute the values of American education, this article has explored how American academia contains within it both equalizing ideals of global and multicultural citizenship that transcend identity, as well as exclusions and elisions that prevent equal access to these ideals. American academia is after all just as foundationally exclusive and elite as it is egalitarian and promoting of merit-based and entrepreneurial forms of success. This duality produces and reconfigures different forms of citizenship as it travels to new places and interacts with local forms of belonging and exclusion. These multiple logics exist in the home spaces of higher education and are not corruptions or dilutions that occur once the university travels, or once the university enters into a new age of millennial capital. While Qatar has its own set of concerns and state entanglements that actors in Education City have to negotiate, it is not a worse or 'not yet' space for liberal education. In fact, some things seemed more open than they were at Texas A&M's home campus, where I was working at the time, like discussions of Palestine or the ability to secure interest-free loans no matter what your national background. The over-whelming pushback from within American academia against projects like Education City needs nuancing through engagement with the on-the-ground complexities of daily life in American branch campuses. It might be important for us to remember in our current discussions of a university in crisis that the language of crisis was also used when women wanted to enter the Western academy, and when programmes like Ethnic Studies and Cultural Studies fought (and continue to fight) for legitimization. What exactly are we 'losing' through the internationalization of our universities, and which actors are centred and which marginalized in the language of loss and gain? In fact, the way in which Qatar and other states are represented in this rhetoric assumes a one-directional benefit: ideas and public good supposedly flow from the USA into spaces that might not yet be deserving of them or unable to handle them properly. But there are many interesting ways in which the branch campus speaks back to the American academy, if it is willing to listen. Perhaps it is in the potential conversations between students in these seemingly disparate places that new, as yet unimagined forms of public good are possible, even within a climate of neo-liberal academic globalization.

Acknowledgements

I would like to thank Peggy Levitt and Pal Nyíri for including me in this special volume and for providing valuable feedback on the article during the review process. Caroline Melly's input on early drafts of the piece was also invaluable, as was feedback from panelists and audience members at the American Anthropology Association meetings in Chicago, the Social Change and Migration in the Gulf Monarchies conference at CERI – Sciences Po, and the University of California Irvine Markets and Money conference.

Funding

The research for this article was funded in part by the Program for the Enhancement of Scholarly and Creative Activities at Texas A&M University.

Notes

1.   Education City has recently been merged into one entity called Hamad bin Khalifa University by the Qatar Foundation. However, it is still commonly referred to as Education City and the branch campuses continue to operate as relatively independent institutions.
2.   For a similar exploration of K-12 education in the UAE, see Vora (2013).
3.   My interview subjects were recruited through email lists of current students and employees at Education City campuses, through word-of-mouth and through snowball sampling. In some cases subjects contacted me because they had heard of my project through peers. Interviews were semi-structured and lasted between forty-five minutes and two hours on average. Only two interviewees were former students, and those interviews did not take place until after the term and grade submission were complete. In all, my interviewees comprised four Qatari students (two men and two women), six foreign resident students (all South Asian and Arab, with the exception of one white American), three faculty members and three administrators. Participant observation took place mainly at TAMUQ, but also at Georgetown, at the Education City student centre and at Carnegie Mellon. I also draw from my own teaching and working experiences here as part of this ethnography.
4.   See, for example, a recent letter from Yale faculty to the American Association of University Professors criticizing Yale's presence in Singapore: http://www.aaup.org/news/2012/open-letter-aaup-yale-community
5.   Lim's argument here is about differences in curricula, aesthetics, financial investment and programming, rather than about which clients branch campuses are aimed at – 'local' or international students.
6.   In addition, the 'local' is a space that is always already cosmopolitan and embedded in transnational 'global' networks, rather than a space to which the global is brought by these institutions.
7.   See also Levitt and Merry (2009) for an exploration of how certain ideas and approaches become understood as global and others as vernacular.

References

Aksan, V. 2010. "How Do We 'Know' the Middle East?" *Review of Middle East Studies* 44 (1): 3–12.
Ali, S. 2010. *Dubai: Gilded Cage*. London: Yale University Press.
Altbach, P. G. 2004a. "Globalisation and the University: Myths and Realities in an Unequal World." *Tertiary Education and Management* 10 (1): 3–25. doi:10.1080/13583883.2004.9967114.
Altbach, P. G. 2004b. "Higher Education Crosses Borders." *Change*, March–April, 2004.
Althusser, Louis. 2006. "Ideology and Ideological State Apparatuses." In *The Anthropology of the State: A Reader*, edited by Aradhana Sharma and Akhil Gupta, 86–111. Malden: Blackwell Publishing.
Apple, Michael. 2004. *Ideology and Curriculum*. New York: Routledge Falmer.
Bertelsen, R. G. 2012. "Private Foreign-Affiliated Universities, the State, and Soft Power: The American University of Beirut and the American University in

Cairo." *Foreign Policy Analysis* 8 (3): 293–311. doi:10.1111/j.1743-8594.2011.00163.x.

Chakrabarty, D. 2000. *Provincializing Europe: Postcolonial Thought and Historical Difference*. Princeton: Princeton University Press.

Collins, James. 2009. "Social Reproduction in Classrooms and Schools." *Annual Review of Anthropology* 38 (1): 33–48. doi:10.1146/annurev.anthro.37.081407.085242.

Gardner, A. 2010. *City of Strangers: Gulf Migration and the Indian Community in Bahrain*. Ithaca, NY: Cornell University Press.

Kane, Tanya. 2012. "Transplanting Education: A Case Study of the Production of 'American-style' Doctors in a Non-American Setting." PhD diss., Social Anthropology, University of Edinburgh.

Kelly, M. 2010. "Issues in the Development of a Gulf Studies Program at the American University of Kuwait: An Ethnograpy." *Review of Middle East Studies* 14 (2): 152–165.

Krieger, Z. 2008. "An Academic Building Boom Transforms the Persian Gulf." *The Chronicle of Higher Education* 54 (29): A26.

Leonard, K. 2003. "South Asian Workers in the Gulf: Jockeying for Places." In *Globalization under Construction*, edited by R. W. Perry and B. Maurer, 129–170. Minneapolis: University of Minnesota Press.

Levinson, Bradley A., Douglas E. Foley, and Dorothy C. Holland, eds. 1996. *The Cultural Production of the Educated Person: Critical Ethnographies of Schooling and Local Practice*. Albany: State University of New York Press.

Levitt, P., and S. Merry. 2009. "Vernacularization on the Ground: Local Uses of Global Women's Rights in Peru, China, India and the United States." *Global Networks* 9 (4): 441–461. doi:10.1111/j.1471-0374.2009.00263.x.

Lim, E.-B. 2009. "Performing the Global University." *Social Text* 27 (4): 25–44. doi:10.1215/01642472-2009-053.

Looser, T. 2012. "The Global University, Area Studies, and the World Citizen: Neoliberal Geography's Redistribution of the 'World.'" *Cultural Anthropology* 27 (1): 97–117. doi:10.1111/j.1548-1360.2012.01128.x.

Lukose, Ritty. 2007. "The Difference that Diaspora Makes: Thinking through the Anthropology of Immigrant Education in the United States." *Anthropology & Education Quarterly* 38 (4): 405–418. doi:10.1525/aeq.2007.38.4.405.

Miller-Idriss, Cynthia, and Elizabeth Hanauer. 2011. "Transnational Higher Education: Offshore Campuses in the Middle East." *Comparative Education* 47 (2): 181–207. doi:10.1080/03050068.2011.553935.

Morey, A. I. 2004. "Globalization and the Emergence of For-Profit Higher Education." *Higher Education* 48 (1): 131–150. doi:10.1023/B:HIGH.0000033768.76084.a0.

Olds, K., and N. Thrift. 2005. "Cultures on the Brink: Reengineering the Soul of Capitalism - on a Global Scale." In *Global Assemblages: Technology, Politics and Ethics as Anthropological Problems*, edited by A. Ong and S. Collier, 270–290. Oxford: Blackwell.

Ong, A. 2006. *Neoliberalism as Exception: Mutations in Citizenship and Sovreignty*. Durham: Duke University Press.

Poovey, M. 2001. "The Twenty-First-Century University and the Market: What Price Economic Viability?" *Differences: A Journal of Feminist Cultural Studies* 12 (1): 1–16.

Rosaldo, R. 1994. "Cultural Citizenship and Educational Democracy." *Cultural Anthropology* 9 (3): 402–411.

Sarroub, Loukia K. 2005. *All American Yemeni Girls: Being Muslim in a Public School.* Philadelphia: University of Pennsylvania Press.

Sidhu, R., K. C. Ho, and B. Yeoh. 2011. "Emerging Education Hubs: The Case of Singapore." *Higher Education* 61 (1): 23–40. doi:10.1007/s10734-010-9323-9.

Slaughter, Sheila, and Gary Rhoades. 2009. *Academic Capitalism and the New Economy: Markets, States, and Higher Education.* Baltimore: Johns Hopkins University Press.

Tetrault, Mary Ann. 2010. "Great Expectations: Western-style Education in the Gulf States." In *Industrialization in the Gulf,* edited by J.-F. Seznec and M. Kirk, eds., 143–154. London: Routledge.

Vora, N. 2008. "Producing Diasporas and Globalization: Indian Middle-Class Migrants in Dubai." *Anthropological Quarterly* 81 (2): 377–406.

Vora, N. 2009. "The Precarious Existence of Dubai's Indian Middle-Class." *Middle East Report* 252: 18–21.

Vora, N. 2013. *Impossible Citizens: Dubai's Indian Diaspora.* Durham, NC: Duke University Press.

Vora, N. forthcoming. "Is the University Universal? Mobile (Re)Constitutions of American Academia in the Gulf Arab States." *Anthropology & Education Quarterly* 46 (1).

Yon, D. A. 2003. "Highlights and Overview of the History of Educational Ethnography." *Annual Review of Anthropology* 32 (1): 411–429. doi:10.1146/annurev.anthro.32.061002.093449.

Tuning in or turning off: performing emotion and building cosmopolitan solidarity in international music competitions

Lisa McCormick

This article suggests that international classical music competitions are becoming sites of the global cultural public sphere. Like post-traditional festivals, they have previously served as arenas where nations compete for supremacy. But as these events become more globalized, they create opportunities to foster cosmopolitan sociability and cultivate global values. Through a discourse analysis of media coverage and online commentary from a selected case, I examine how difference is constructed in the competition context and how these categories complicate attempts to relate musically across differences. This analysis highlights the central role of emotion in the process of cultural inclusion, both as a discursive trope in evaluations of musical authenticity and as a signifier of value justifying the incorporation of a wider range of people into the circle of great musicians.

Delanty (2011) casts the festival phenomenon as an expression of cosmopolitanism and a site of the global cultural public sphere. Events such as art biennales and literature festivals have proliferated in Europe and beyond, establishing a distinctive genre of cultural experience where attendees are both consumers and participants in a space and time of 'concentrated debate and "collective effervescence"' (Delanty 2011, 195). These are 'post-traditional' festivals where the distinction between high and popular culture is blurred, and the lively spirit of carnival permeates the high culture domain. Initially, arts festivals supplanted the local and national orientations of traditional state-run occasions by introducing an international framework that made the event an arena for nations to compete. But as the national context has diminished, the cultural logic of festivals has shifted towards cosmopolitanism, providing models for 'connecting global issues to particular contexts' and creating 'moments of openness, exchange and dialogue' (196). These moments highlight the cultural dimension of global citizenship by raising issues of representation (e.g. of race, ethnicity and gender) and of access, both to the creative realm and to the wider political community.

I wish to consider whether international classical music competitions are also sites of the global cultural public sphere despite an international framework that suggests resistance to the cultural logic of cosmopolitanism. Competitions might seem too different to make this equation justifiable. While they describe themselves as 'celebration[s] dedicated to a particular discipline or disciplines of music', they serve a gatekeeping function; an international jury awards prizes to 'the most outstanding' competitors, prizes intended to gain 'for the award-winners widespread recognition that helps further their careers'.[1] This aside, however, competitions resemble festivals in several significant respects. First, they are spaces where 'the local and the global interact' (Delanty 2011, 197). Competitions draw musicians from around the world to participate, but they are run by small organizations that depend on the local musical infrastructure (orchestras, concert halls and volunteers). Attendees therefore identify simultaneously with the hosting locality and the broader music community.

Second, sociability is an integral part of audience experience. Sassatelli (2011, 21) thinks it a mistake to measure the vibrancy and relevance of festivals only in terms of economic effects, finding cultural significance in their reorganization of urban space to create informal spaces for debate and criticism. Competitions share this discursive quality. The competitive format provides opportunity for audiences to become culture-debating publics, provoking them to consider the qualities of effective musical performance and to question the basis for aesthetic authority. On a more fundamental level, the contradiction between the competition's unifying and divisive functions – its dual nature as celebration and sorting mechanism –inspires both dissent and advocacy among participants. These two features make competitions sites of the global cultural public sphere, but the real litmus test for their cosmopolitanism is their transformative character. If they are occasions in which the self is transformed 'in light of the encounter with the other', competitions cultivate the form of cosmopolitanism that is 'more than the simple condition of internationalism or globality', or, for that matter, consumerism (Delanty 2011).

Granted, the competition format is not unknown in the festival genre. Most film festivals are competitive, some to the extent that several prizes are determined by audience vote in addition to those awarded by jury. The competitive feature has unfortunately helped ground a critique of the 'festival as cultural public sphere' thesis from a Bourdieuian perspective. According to English (2011, 64), 'the festival is as much a field for the competitive accumulation and more-or-less exploitative deployment of symbolic capital as it is a form for the exchange of ideas and construction of reasoned consensus about art and society'; the competition format simply makes the 'consecratory role' more obvious. He concludes that the processes of valuation and judgement institutionalized through the film festival circuit have a distorting effect that is exaggerated in the case of African cinema.

However, the lopsided apparatus of selection, classification and promotion that English maps in the film festival circuit does not carry over to international music competitions. They inhabit a transnational institutional space overseen by the World Federation of International Music Competitions, a regulatory meta-organization founded in 1957 to define and enforce professional standards.[2] Here again we find the intersection of the local and the global; the Federation's membership consists of city-based organizations from thirty-seven countries. For historical reasons, the Federation's 122 members are mainly based in Europe, but competitions from peripheral and emerging musical centres are steadily placing themselves on this cultural 'map' by obtaining membership.

Elsewhere (McCormick, Forthcoming), I argue that music competitions serve as sites for cultural inclusion by virtue of their status as civil institutions of the aesthetic sphere. Competitions were typically founded by charismatic figures to protest or supplement existing opportunity structures in the music world; they developed into more permanent bureaucratic organizations but retained relative autonomy from established musical institutions such as national conservatories, professional orches-tras and government agencies. A Bourdieuian sociology cannot adequately explain the role of competitions in the music world. It is difficult to argue that they serve as distributors of symbolic capital because musicians and arts administrators generally doubt their effectiveness as a mechanism for identifying talent; even music industry insiders struggle to identify prizes awarded in recent years that were decisive in establishing international performing careers. And yet professionals and audiences continue to be deeply engaged, suggesting that there is still something important at stake.

Competitions have always enhanced their prestige through the parti-cipation of prominent musicians as directors and jury members, but their legitimacy is increasingly grounded in legal-rational rather than aesthetic terms. Musicians today expect competitions to be rule-regulated rather than arbitrary, with transparent regulations applied consistently. The intervention of civil ideals into the world of music can be found in both the measures adopted voluntarily by competition administrators, such as requiring that jurors abstain from voting for their own students, and in the bitter denunciations expounded by their harshest critics, including the initiative called '10,000 Musicians Against Corruption in Music Competi-tions' (Duchen 2009). But it would be wrong to see this as a reform movement responding to specific problems; rather, the aesthetic and civil spheres are fundamentally incompatible, and participants must continually negotiate the contradictions between fairness and objectivity on the one hand, and beauty and excellence on the other.

The civil qualities that enable competitions to become sites of cultural inclusion are openness and inclusiveness.[3] Competitions are open about how they operate and they stage events that are open to the public. They are inclusive in that musicians of every nationality, ethnic origin, religion and gender can compete; competition organizations also seek to expand the audience and the available forms of participation through ancillary programming, outreach initiatives and communications technologies.[4] I will argue that the relational practices that follow from the implementation of civil ideals not only create the conditions for a critical-debating public to emerge; they also foster cosmopolitanism. When musicians from around the world gather to perform a diverse repertoire in front of an international jury and a heterogeneous audience, cosmopolitanism is not just represented – it is performed.

To this end, I follow Glick Schiller et al. (2011, 402) who ground the abstract notion of cosmopolitanism by identifying 'concrete social practices and "ways of being"'. Drawing from Simmel, they propose the concept of 'cosmopolitan sociability' to refer to the 'forms of competence and communication skills that are based on the human capacity to create social relations of inclusiveness and openness to the world' (402). In the competition context, one source of this cosmopolitan sensibility is the repertoire list. By including non-canonical works, and by making compulsory the performance of a newly commissioned work, competitions require aspiring musicians to explore difference and to develop a cosmopolitan competence in a wider range of music, incorporating elements from musical traditions (popular, non-Western, ethnic) that are not standard in conservatory training. Because competitors are more likely to programme these works in their future concerts, competitions help to expand the Western classical music canon.

In addition to this cosmopolitan musical competence, competitions encourage communication skills among competitors and audience members from diverse cultural backgrounds. Competitions create an occasion where music community, general public and media gather to 'heighten the appreciation of the repertory, performance tradition, history, and culture' of classical music, providing an arena where collective identities can be refashioned and allegiances extended beyond national boundaries.[5] This extension requires the generation of solidarity. As Alexander (2013, 536) argues, the form of solidarity depends on the construction of difference: 'The more civil the solidarity, the more likely that feelings of connection can be extended to include apparently different others.' While Alexander emphasizes meaning and emotions as key issues in civil societies, Nash explores the affective dimension of cosmopolitan citizenship. In her analysis of the 'Make Poverty History' campaign, culture is as important as legal and political structures in making global citizenship a reality. Here again the extension of allegiances is key: 'As an intersubjectively recognized status, citizenship is reflexive, containing the logical and practical possibility of reaching beyond itself, beyond existing schedules of rights and responsibilities to create new relationships' (Nash 2008, 168).

Music competitions operate outside the 'cosmopolitanizing state', but they still provide an institutional context where new relationships can be forged and feelings of connection generated. This possibility is engaged when competitor performances convince listeners of a common ground of shared human experience without requiring the elimination or bracketing of cultural difference. Audience members must fulfill their side of the bargain by being open to alternative interpretive approaches and by challenging fellow listeners whose convictions undermine conviviality or whose interactional modes threaten civility.

Through a discourse analysis of competition commentary, I will examine how constructions of difference, namely race and ethnicity, interact with the transnational quality of the contemporary musical social field and the multicultural identity of its participants. The conventional categories used by journalists and audience members create problems for competitors who do not fit neatly within them or who deliberately traverse them. But the very attempt to cross these boundaries, successful or not, raises the issue of musically relating across differences. My analysis will also show that emotion is central to the performative success of these cosmopolitan ventures, serving as either barrier or bridge to global citizenship. But first I will discuss developments in the world of music that have brought issues of racial and ethnic identity to the fore.

Changing demographics in classical music

For decades, international music competitions were overshadowed by Cold War politics. Classical music was a field in which the Soviet bloc sought to demonstrate a cultural supremacy that the West was determined to contest. Today, the geopolitical referent for the 'East' reflects instead the strong presence of Asians and Asian immigrants in the classical music world. Chinese and Japanese musicians have won top prizes at competitions since the 1950s, but in the last twenty years their presence within the ranks of competitors has risen from 21% to more than 35% (Johnson 2009). This trend is unsurprising given the demographic composition of music schools. For example, at the Juilliard School of Music, a prestigious conservatory in New York City, Koreans have outnumbered other foreign students three to one since the 1980s (cited in Yang 2007). A professor at the Eastman School of Music in Rochester suggested that 'the piano departments of the major schools in the United States would close if it weren't for the Asian students' (Cantrell 2005, 1G). But Asians do not have to go abroad to study classical music. *The Economist* estimates that between 30 and 100 million children in China are learning to play piano or violin; enrolment at the Sichuan Conservatory in Chengdu alone exceeds 14,000 students (N.A. 2013).

According to Yang (2007), Western classical music has thrived in East Asia through a combination of state support and cultural change. Orchestras and conservatories funded in the post-war period to advance modern nation-building provided an infrastructure for an expanding middle class to embrace 'foreign music as a marker of social distinction' (Yang 2007, 3). In China's case, the position of Western classical music was improved after the Cultural Revolution by the strengthening of relations with Eastern Europe and the USSR; Soviet musicians were invited to teach in the conservatories, reinforcing pedagogical and interpretive styles established decades earlier by émigrés escaping the Russian Revolution (Kraus 1989, 79). The status of Western classical music in East Asia contributes to its popularity among Asian immigrants; studying Western classical music promises a 'stable cultural link' to the host country without implying rejection of the native country (Yang 2007, 11). For Yang, international music competitions bolstered the rise of Western classical music in East Asia in two ways. First, they codified an international standard for Asian musicians to measure themselves vis-à -vis their Euro-American counterparts. Second, the prizes served as a form of 'cultural validation' (3). The analysis that follows aims to offer deeper insight into how the core group extends this recognition, although it will be cast in terms of inclusion rather than validation.

Case and method

The data to be examined are drawn from two cycles of a particular competition, the Cliburn International Piano Competition. This narrow view affords greater sensitivity to contextual factors that figure into interaction; for example, scheduling affects the pacing of developments and the urgency of debates. The aim is not to generalize from this single case, but to gain insight into key issues and to achieve conceptual clarity for operationalization in further studies.

The Cliburn is a representative case in the most important respect: it conforms to Federation-mandated procedures. It is also recognized as one of 'bigger' competitions in terms of its financial resources, reputation and role in shaping the mission of the Federation in recent decades. It was founded to honour Van Cliburn, whose victory at the 1958 Tchaikovsky Competition in Moscow transformed the pianist into a Cold War 'double hero'; for Americans, he was the 'American Sputnik' outperforming the Russians in a cultural realm where Russians had excelled, while for the

Soviets, his triumph resonated with Khrushchev's idea of 'peaceful coexistence'. The Cliburn competition has been held every four years since 1962, attracting young (age eighteen to thirty) pianists from around the world to Fort Worth, Texas. While repertoire requirements have changed over the years, the tripartite format has remained; a first elimination reduces the candidate field from thirty-five to twelve, a second elimination further reduces it to six, ending in a final concerto round. The three winners receive a generous cash award,[6] but musicians consider the rest of the prize package to be more valuable – a professional recording opportunity, three years of management and the publicity surrounding the event.

That publicity reverberates much wider than the classical music world itself. Competitions are 'media events' (Dayan and Katz 1992) staged for a general public; performances are broadcast and developments covered in newspapers and specialist music publications. Like many of its peer organizations, the Cliburn Foundation adopted new digital technologies to expand its audience and the forms of engagement available to them.[7] Since 2005, sessions have been broadcast live over the internet; in 2009, 123,000 unique users from 150 countries logged in to watch the competition.[8] The official website includes an interactive weblog that invites competition followers attending in person or listening to the broadcast to share their reactions and respond to reviews posted by 'official bloggers'. Weblogs being a relatively new genre of computer-mediated communication, the 2005 Cliburn blog accumulated only 836 comments over the seventeen days of the competition; but in 2009, 6,298 comments were posted. This was sometimes an outlet for fan activity, expressing enthusiasm for the Cliburn or intense attachments to particular players; but blog participants were more critics than consumers. In comments as long as 800 words, they debated a range of issues, including the merits of particular performances, the fairness of the rules, the implications of jury decisions and the future of Western classical music.

Like face-to-face discussions, online interactions take the form of sociability in Simmel's (1971) sense of the term: they revolve around shared interests that are not strictly utilitarian. But this sociability is only cosmopolitan to the extent that it fosters 'social relationships that do not negate cultural, religious or gendered differences but see people as capable of relationships of experiential commonalities despite differences' (Glick Schiller et al. 2011). To assess this openness to difference, I investigated how race and ethnicity appeared in competition discourse, concentrating on the 'old' and 'new' media sources from the Cliburn's 2005 and 2009 cycles. Newspaper coverage presented competitors as representatives of groups by classifying them according to chosen social characteristics. For example, in 2005, gender was highlighted over nationality when the initial selection of competitors drew the headline 'Cliburn's feminine tone: Female artists dominate a once macho piano contest' (Gay 2005) and the first elimination results were reported as 'Record number of women make semifinals' (Autrey 2005b). In contrast, the 2009 cycle emphasized disability and race with headlines such as 'Blind pianist shares top Van Cliburn prize' (Mangan 2009) and 'Asian pianists sweep Van Cliburn competition' (Zeeble 2009). The second data source, blog postings, reveals how these categories were picked up by the competition audience and incorporated into their evaluation of competitors' performances.

That blog users are a self-selected group does not negate the advantage of this data source being naturally occurring talk; unlike focus groups or interviews, artificial situations where researchers cannot avoid imposing categories, blogs record experiences in real time and in the subjects' chosen setting (Potter 2002). Cultural structures can be reconstructed through blogs because postings are public statements that invoke shared symbolic frameworks for comprehensibility and persuasiveness. Blogs are becoming a standard feature of the competition experience. As communication technologies become a more prevalent mode for engaging with the arts,[9] and as online and offline interactions become more intertwined, qualitative researchers must 'expand the methodological toolbox to better capture this social reality' (Beneito-Montagut 2011, 717).

My discussion below focuses on the official Cliburn blogs because they provided a central hub for competition followers for the entire duration of each cycle. Several blog users mentioned threads on other online forums, such as the 'great-pianists group' on Yahoo!, 'Piano World forum' and the 'Cliburn 2009' Google group, and often reported the consensus – or lack thereof – in these other spaces. To trace the degree of openness and inclusiveness in the core group's discourse, I focused on online sources in the dominant language of the competition's host country. While the resultant picture is partial, it highlights how 'emotion', a context-dependent category, becomes problematized in this setting. In the Anglophone West, emotion is commonly coded as polluting in debate and deliberation but highly desirable in artistic performance. While we would expect structural differentiation to keep aesthetic and civil spheres distinct, competitions straddle both domains by implementing rationalized procedures to recognize artistic excellence. Here aesthetic judgements are not purely subjective because the awarding of a prize constitutes a claim of universal worth; taste preferences normally grounded in personal inclinations must satisfy the standards of moral-practical arguments. Jury members negotiate competing cultural commitments to these realms in their official capacity, but the same contradiction is found among blog participants who enter voluntarily into debates about who deserves to win. We can observe in their discourse the struggle to make reasoned and unbiased arguments about their personal response to performances, and how under certain conditions claims on behalf of performers raise the issue of generalized cultural inclusion.

Subsequent research might explore whether emotion is similarly problematized in discussions about the Cliburn in another language community, such as 'forumklassika.ru', Russia's largest classical music portal. Another direction for further research is a comparison with non-Western contexts. Would a piano competition held in China that included Chinese composers in the required repertoire list change the context of meaning-creation regarding the emotionality of performance and its relative value? While this study explores how mastery over, authenticity in and ownership of classical music is constructed with reference to an American context, further empirical investigation is needed to reveal how these issues can come into conflict with nationalist discourses foregrounding 'indigenous' art traditions in emerging musical centres.

Discussion

In international music competitions, competitors enter as individuals, not as official representatives of a country.[10] The international framework remains engaged nonetheless because competitors are identified by their citizenship in press releases and programmes. With no official national quotas, the number of countries 'represented' varies from cycle to cycle. Organizations report this figure to the Federation to demonstrate that they are international in more than name by attracting contenders from outside the host country.[11] The world of classical music involves a second layer of national political identification; the establishment of national conservatories across Europe in the nineteenth century crystallized distinctive approaches to musical expression and instrumental technique that became conventionally identified as 'national schools' (Ritterman 2002). While teachers and students have always been more mobile than these categories presume, the tally of competitors from a given country remains a standard measure of a national school's strength. For example:

> Amid a sea of young Asian and Slavic virtuosos, the Italians stand out... No native-born German made it into the field of 35, nor any French, Austrians or Poles. This year, Italy has the stranglehold on Old Europe's bragging rights. Somewhere in musical heaven, Beethoven is pulling his hair and Chopin is fainting in shame. But Verdi couldn't be prouder. (Autrey 2005a, 1A)

For most of the twentieth century, Russian competitors dominated the top ranks of the competition circuit, and a reporter covering the 2005 Cliburn admitted surprise in learning that China was 'the biggest supplier of pianists' that year (Cantrell 2005). Four years later, media commentary revisited the subverted expectation of Russian dominance. Under the headline 'Where are all the Russians?', Marton (2009) answered with a narrative of the Russian piano school's decline:

In the past, when it came time to determine which nationality all but dominated the list of pianists entering the [Cliburn], a 1966 film easily summed up the answer: "The Russians Are Coming, the Russians Are Coming." Over the past 20 years, Russian pianists have made up no fewer than four and, in 1997, a field-dominating 11, of the 30 or so Cliburn competitors. And that profusion of Russian players has often produced a Russian... as the gold-medal winner. *This year, that flow of Russian talent has all but dried up.* Of the 30 competitors to play in the preliminary round, only two hail from Russia. And *those spots traditionally penciled-in for Russians have been occupied by China*, with seven players, and seven players in total from Korea and Japan. (Marton 2009, AA05, emphasis added)

Further undermining nationality as a useful identifier, some competitors carry dual citizenship or are naturalized citizens. They can be lumped into 'contingents' only by supplementing the international framework with another regional layer:

Rounding out the Far Eastern contingent are two South Koreans and another Korean native now a citizen of the United States. By contrast, Russia... is supplying six competitors, and another has joint Russian and German citizenship. Counting the naturalized Chinese and Korean natives, the US has five entrants. (Cantrell 2005, 1G)

On the Cliburn blog, the thin showing by Russian pianists did not go unnoticed. One blogger confessed: 'I really miss the Russians... All of those pianists who trained, from birth (!), in the Russian system played at the highest qualities and with the most solid school.'[12] But the sudden increase in Chinese competitors prompted more heated discussion. Blog users converged on 'the rise of China' narrative to frame that cycle of the competition, but split on whether the People's Republic should be seen as threat or saviour:

China has something like 20 million young pianists waiting to be the next Lang Lang and Yuja Wang. What we hear at Fort Worth is just the tip of the iceberg. Kong Xiang Dong (a former Bachauer winner) owns something like a hundred piano schools all over China, all teaching Western music. He was able to assemble a mass piano concert in Shanghai with something like 2000 pianists playing together. Certainly gives a new dimension to the Cold War dictum "We will bury you"[13]
It's a darn shame that not a single pianist from the Americas (North, Central and South) was chosen for the semi[final round]. I recently read that there are 30 million Chinese youngsters taking piano lessons and 3–5 million are taking it very seriously. Soon, China will become the mecca for pianists in the same vein that she is now the mecca for table-tennis enthusiasts. Apparently, the younger generation in China with the encouragement and support from the Chinese government, is going all out for western classical music while youngsters here in the west indulge themselves in other kinds

of so-called "music". I wouldn't be the least bit surprised that in Cliburn competitions ten or twenty years down the road, all the semi and finalists are from Asia with Chinese pianists in the dominating role.[14]
[W]hy knock the Chinese? If they take on the mantle of great traditions from the West, then we need to thank our lucky stars that "classical music" (especially piano music) has a bright future after all.[15]

These excerpts demonstrate that once candidates are discursively con-structed as representatives of social groups, the music competition becomes an arena where the boundaries of the musical civil sphere can be questioned and the possibility of their expansion is engaged. For boundaries to be redrawn – as the third blog user phrased it, for the 'mantle of great traditions' to be extended – members of the core group must be communicatively convinced that out-groups deserve this trust and respect. Competition performances can serve as claims for cultural inclusion because they afford a multilayered demonstration of civil competence; through their performances on and off the stage, musicians embody the qualities, orientations and skills required for full participation in the musical realm and beyond. They demonstrate the capacity for self-criticism by volunteering to participate in this very public form of evaluation. By following the rules outlined by the organization and accepting the outcome of the deliberation process, competitors display respect for the rule of law. Within the bounds of playing by the rules, they show self-motivation and individuality in how they approach the satisfac-tion of requirements. They display openness to difference in their selection of repertoire. But it is through the embodiment of musical qualities (see Table 1) that competitors have the greatest impact on the public construction of collective identities on which the incorporation process depends. I will now retrace how the binary oppositions relating to emotion and authenticity are invoked once racial and ethnic difference gains currency as a principal concern.

The Cliburn no longer imposes a repertoire list for recital rounds. Despite this programming freedom, competitors understandably gravitate to pieces that showcase pianism in terms that judges and audience are most likely to appreciate, through canonical works that epitomize universalism (e.g. Beethoven, Mozart, Schumann) or celebrated works by 'national' composers (e.g. Chopin, Bartók, Rachmaninoff). Competitors who stay within this tried-and-true repertoire remain limited to the form and extent of cosmopolitanism as it was musically expressed in an age of colonialism, which includes its Orientalist and exoticist versions (see Born and Hesmondhalgh 2000). Few pianists opt to display their sophistication by programming non-Western and experimental composers because they risk straying too far from standard measures of excellence.

Apart from the commissioned work by a contemporary American composer, pianists can select repertoire that will play to their strengths.

Table 1. The binary discourse of musical qualities.

Musical	Unmusical
Original	Derivative
Authentic	Inauthentic
Natural	Contrived/perverse
Profound	Superficial
Sincere	Manipulative/calculated
Passionate	Emotionless/mechanical

Despite its open appearance, this arrangement does not necessarily put competitors on an equal footing. An association with an esteemed national school through an ethnically identifiable name coupled with the distinctive instrumental technique in the appropriate repertoire can give competitors a certain stylistic authority. For example:

> This Rachmaninoff sonata is real Rachmaninoff playing – it [is] deep, soulful, Russian playing. I hear Rachmaninoff in this playing. ... [Ilya Rashkovskiy] is clearly stands (sic) in a distinguished Russian line. I'm sure Krainev, and Neuhaus (somewhere…) are proud.[16]

In contrast, several blog posts suggested that listeners were more likely to find performances inauthentic when a pianist's ethnicity or training did not align with the nationalist repertoire programmed:

> What a pitty (sic) there is a czech (sic) composer in the semis and noone (sic) now could hear it played by the czech pianist… that is really wierd (sic) at least[17]
> [Soyeon Lee's] afternoon program: the first book of Albéniz' *Iberia*, and Schumann's *Carnival*. For my taste, I thought the Albeniz could have exuded a little more Latin charm. It felt a little too restrained.[18]
> I like everything Feng Zhang plays, except the Rachmaninoff 2nd Sonata; I just don't hear the Russian essence, soul and nuances of other past contestants who played in 2005 and 2001. I believe "Russian" is an area he can improve on, if you give him a few more years.[19]

The bridging of perceived cultural distance is a problem of performance, but it is not insurmountable. When the performer succeeds in musically 'taking the role of the other', a reciprocal identification with the audience can grow into solidarity. Van Cliburn inspired this cultural extension at the 1958 Tchaikovsky Competition in Moscow when he performed cherished Russian repertoire in a manner that was compelling to the Soviet music public. This musical gesture allowed the Soviet public to 'see themselves' in an American pianist despite Cold War hostilities, and the collective effervescence generated by this identification was affirmed when the jury awarded Van Cliburn first prize. Fifty years later in Fort Worth, a similar cultural extension is in evidence when observers of an American competition describe a Russian pianist as 'show[ing] Americans what freedom is',[20] declare a Japanese pianist 'born to play Beethoven',[21] or compare a Chinese pianist favourably to iconic interpreters of the Western classical canon:

> If I didn't know the Beethoven was played by Haochen, I would have thought it must be a performance by Brendel thirty years ago, his Chopin by Pollini or Ashkenzay in their heydays and his Stravinsky by that amazing Russian Nicolai Petrof years back…[22]

As this last excerpt suggests, it is not always the nationalist repertoire that secures a cultural extension; stylistic flexibility can be equally worthy of admiration. Concert pianists are expected to be comfortable in many styles, so competitions build this into their requirements; the extent of each pianist's musical cosmopolitanism must be displayed over the course of the event.

In order for cultural extensions to succeed, performers must convince the audience that they have not only *understood* the musical style on an intellectual level but that they *felt* it. Authenticity in this context has a double sense referring both to the performer's knowledge of a musical tradition and their ability to embody the affective dimension of this understanding in a sincere manner. If the pianist seems to be going through the motions, performative 'fusion' (Alexander 2004) is only partially achieved and listeners are left unsatisfied. On the Cliburn blog, competition followers described this reaction in forms ranging from disappointment to anger:

> Her playing reminded of an actor who could act the part but never be the part.[23]
> Yeol Eum Son seems to play note-perfect but for some reason her music is not speaking to me so far…[24]
> This rachmaninoff (sic) is very disconnected and I'm having a hard time paying attention to his playing. Not memorable in any way, in my opinion. He is destroying this beautiful, beautiful music!!![25]

The ability to convey emotion is prized in pianists because this enables the listener to achieve a heightened state. As Hennion (2001) has shown, music lovers often adopt a discourse similar to that of drug addicts to describe the transcendence sought in musical experience. Accordingly, they are disappointed by performances that are perceived as emotionally empty:

> A controlled, relatively accurate performance of the piece… but *he just never took me over the edge*. He's definitely talented, but *I kept waiting to*

be knocked off my chair, and it didn't happen. For certain works, this being one of them, *we need to feel the pianist left their "guts" on the floor*!! (well, not literally of course)[26]

For several who posted on the Cliburn blog, the negative effect of emotionless performance cancelled out any enthusiasm about an impressive display of technical facility:

> ...*he played like an engineer* and not an artist. Lots of perfection, but *depth of soul was missing*...[27]
> Brilliant, and so so *cold*. I feel sorry for the guy as a human, but he sure can play.[28]
> ...If a singer were to mimic her phrasing there, he or she would feel *like a robot*...[29]

The positive coding of emotion in these passages introduces an intriguing paradox. In musical settings, emotion is the catalyst for generating a solidarity that provides momentum for the incorporation process and the subsequent expansion of the musical public. But in theories of the public sphere, emotion is an uncivil quality that disqualifies individuals from participation in public life, and this coding is reflected in civil discourse (Alexander 2006). The key to resolving this apparent contradiction can be found by considering the metaphors chosen by blog users to denigrate emotionless playing. In describing pianists as 'machines' capable of 'pixel-perfect playing', or by introducing colourful nicknames like 'the Undertaker',[30] listeners are suggesting that these musicians are desensitized.

The most common response to performances executed by seemingly 'insensitive' musicians is boredom. For example:

> All of this repertoire was played with a certain drab sameness, even the Ligeti which I was looking forw... to... ZZZZzzzz......[31]

Occasionally listeners concede that emotional detachment suits the piece being performed:

> His morose and necrotic personality fits this "witchy" piece to a T. He truly let out the depth of his sociopathy here and quite frankly it was "realer than real." Whatever his thought process and back story to achieve these results worked. This was truly "Jeffrey Dahmer plays Ravel" at its best.[32]

These performances might be memorable and provoke strong reactions, but they fail as claims for cultural inclusion. The inability to feel emotion is as much a disqualifier from public life as irrationality; the core group of the musical public sphere cannot be convinced that out-group members are trustworthy if they doubt their humanity. But if emotion is authentically conveyed through performance – in the double sense of being appropriate to the musical work's style and honestly presented – listeners can share an aspect of human experience with the competitor. Performers with superior communication skills can use this common ground to stimulate deep emotional responses in listeners and help a fragmented audience achieve a degree of unification.

Few pianists enjoy having their playing described as machine-like and robotic, but this is especially damaging for Asian players because it engages the 'neo-Orientalist image of the automaton, the work machine without imagination or soul' (Yang 2007, 14). On the blog, technical facility and artistry were often presented in terms of a trade-off, but the former was no substitute for the latter:

> Not the most dazzling technique... but full of eloquence and that quality (beloved of amateur listeners like me!) of "soul". I though[t] she was a thoroughly "Russian" player (and interestingly she was actually born in Russia, not Ukraine), in that long tradition.[33]
> Most inspired, musicaly (sic) inclined Asian candidate so far?? That's the way I feel. Thoughts??[34]
> Some said earlier the future will bring Asian domination of Classical music. Though improved, I still hear the tendency (in MOST but NOT ALL) towards technical over artistic expression. They'll dominate only if jurors are mostly Asian (and their biases towards technical and Asian will lend a hand) or they as a group, continue to improve artistically...[35]

One difficulty in debating musical performance is that reasoned arguments have their limit; it is impossible to convince someone that they should or should not have been moved by a performance. Nonetheless, civil norms were enforced in the online discussion forum. Anyone was entitled to an opinion, regardless of musical training, so long as reasoned arguments were presented. Two incidents on the Cliburn blog demonstrated that generalizations on the basis of race or ethnicity were not acceptable for judging performance. The first incident was triggered by the following comment, which addresses the issue of emotion discussed above:

> I'm having the strangest feeling about Zhang Haochen's Beethoven. On one level, I am finding his overall performance perfect. On a complete different level, I'm finding it a bit too perfect. Every single crescendo, every single ritardando is being executed with pinpoint accuracy; it's as if he's trying to manufacture emotion via algorithmic efficiency. You know what they say about politicians: "If you can fake sincerity, you've got it made." Anybody else feel this way, or am I out in left field?[36]

Within minutes, there was a terse reply: 'It's [be]cause he's Asian, isn't it? How dare you.'[37] The accusation of 'manufacturing emotion' did not just group together several unmusical qualities; it amplified their negative effect. Responding to the charge of racism, the blog user insisted that no generalizations were being made, only observations pertaining to the one candidate:

> Erm... no, it's not, and I didn't feel this way about any of the other umpteen competitors from Asia who have already gone. For the record, I happen to be Asian myself.[38]

The blog user's racial self-identification aside, vindication was achieved when several other observers in rapid succession confirmed the original impression, and the matter was dropped:

> Nail on the head – *it lacks "real" involvement and appears to be quite calculated* – but there again, he is 19... ...With all this control, though, I would wager the Stravinsky will be very good...[39]
> i just feel that no matter how beautiful his playing is (and it has been thus far), I'm unaffected by it.[40]
> His Chopin missed something for me too and may have been *too mechanically perfect in some parts*. Perhaps, given time he may yet get it.[41]

In the second incident, controversy erupted when a blog user said this of a Bulgarian candidate's performance of Chopin's Piano Concerto No. 1:

> To me it's all Euro-trash !! SORRY !![42]

This reverses the automaton epithet; overdone emotion undermines sincerity from the other direction. Some dismissed this comment as juvenile: 'As for the Euro-trash comment, well (sic) all I have to say is 'Grow up, America !'[43] But other blog users reacted more strongly:

> gnwelch – thanks for the intelligent, well thought-out comment. If you can't construct a cohesively written paragraph as to what YOU don't appreciate (or may[be] don't understand??) about the performance, then perhaps you should withold (sic) such inane comments[44]
> gnwelch, the term "Euro-trash" is an ethnic slur. (Look it up in the dictionary, I just did). If someone did not enjoy a performance by Son, Tsujii, Wu or Zhang, it would be unthinkable to post a comment with an ethnic slur about Asian people and it should be not be different for a performer from Europe or anywhere else. No matter how much you disliked Bozhanov's performance, *that kind of language has no place here in my opinion*.[45]

Both incidents show forum participants intervening to reinforce civil norms. But while the debating public might not tolerate overt racial or ethnic bias in musical judgements, these become more likely to surface once competitors have been culturally constructed into representatives of racial or ethnic group. For some of these groups, a claim for cultural inclusion will be at stake.

Conclusion

Throughout the twentieth century, international music competitions served as an arena where European nations or Cold War superpowers competed for supremacy. But as more aspects of these events become globalized – participating musicians, repertoire performed, evaluation frameworks and audience expectations – they are becoming sites of global citizenship creation. This paper focused on how emotion functions as a discursive trope in evaluations and as a signifier of value justifying the incorporation of a wider range of people into the circle of great musicians. The cosmopolitanization of classical music is more than a mere condition of globality because of its potentially transformative character; to use Delanty's phrase, the self can be transformed in light of the encounter with the other. In the case of performers, this encounter consisted of musically 'taking the role of the other' in works that are culturally distant. For the audience, it consisted of listening to a performance and perceiving it as authentic in a double sense of the term; in addition to honouring the stylistic accuracy of the interpretation, they are moved by its substance and the sincerity of its enactment. Competitions can therefore be said to act as mediators of cosmopolitanism by creating occasions for what Schütz (1951, 92) called 'tuning in'; through music, participants synchronize 'inner time' and experience the "'' We" which is at the foundation of all possible communication'.

Notes

1. WFIMC Recommendations, Article 1.1.
2. The Federation does not oversee the field by keeping a directory of all existing organizations but by serving as standard bearer, consultant and, occasionally, mediator in disputes.
3. I draw from the binary discourse of civil society in Alexander (2006, 57–59). Openness is a quality of civil relations. Others are: trusting, critical, honourable, altruistic, truthful, straightforward, deliberative and friendly. Inclusiveness is a quality of civil institutions, along with: rule-regulated, law, equality, impersonal, contracts, groups and office. Uncivil qualities are defined in opposition to these terms.
4. Age is the only acceptable basis for discrimination. The Federation allows competitions to 'establish minimum and maximum age requirements for competitors'. While the suggested age limit varies by discipline, the age minimum does not; competitors must be at least fifteen years old. WFIMC Recommendations, Article 2.2.
5. WFIMC Recommendations, Article 1.2.
6. In 2009, first, second and third prizewinners received US$20,000.

7.   The goal of audience expansion is not to increase profits. Only not-for-profit organizations qualify for Federation membership.

8.   '2009 Webcast & Media' Cliburn News. Special Issue No. 95, Summer 2009, p. 2. Fort Worth: Van Cliburn Foundation. (Archived at Texas Christian University.).

9.   A survey conducted by the National Endowment for the Arts found that 71% of American adults use electronic media to access the arts (NEA 2012).

10.   During the Cold War, Soviet competitors were effectively official representatives because the government only issued visas to musicians selected through state-controlled channels. Similar practices were temporarily adopted by Chinese officials after the Cultural Revolution (see Kraus 1989).

11.   The Federation's expectation regarding international character extends to the jury. The majority of judges are supposed to 'represent nationalities and countries of residence other than the country in which the competition is held' (WFIMC Statutes, Article 12p.)

12.   Marcus Cato, Cliburn blog, June 7, 2009.

13.   Chang Tou Liang (Singapore), May 24, 2009.

14.   joey c, May 27, 2009.

15.   George Kiorpes, May 27, 2009.

16.   Marcus Cato, May 25, 2009.

17.   Mariana, May 29, 2009.

18.   Hawley, May 23, 2009.

19.   Ho, May 25, 2009.

20.   Jennifer, June 4, 2005.

21.   Eric Zuber, June 7, 2009.

22.   joey c, May 25, 2009.

23.   M. Han, May 27, 2009.

24.   DR, May 26, 2009.

25.   GK, May 30, 2009.

26.   Tom M, May 30, 2009.

27.   Marcus Cato, May 25, 2009.

28.   wr, May 24, 2009.

29.   Mike Winter, May 25, 2005.

30.   Paco, June 580 5, 2005.

31.   Mike Hawley, May 25, 2009.

32.   Paco, June 5, 2005.

33.   AGB, May 23, 2009.

34.   Robert Lee, May 26, 2009.

35.   Jack, May 27, 2009.

36.   The Project, May 25, 2009.

37.   Frank, May 25, 2009.

38.   The Project, May 25, 2009.

39.   Tom, May 25, 2009.

40.   Jeff, May 25, 2009.

41.   Steven Lagerberg, May 25, 2009.

42.   gnwelch, June 3, 2009.

43.   Anne S., June 3, 2009.

44.   Tom, June 3, 2009.

45.   Lily, June 3, 2009.45.

References

Alexander, J. C. 2004. "Cultural Pragmatics: Social Performance between Ritual and Strategy." *Sociological Theory* 22 (4): 527–573. doi:10.1111/j.0735-2751.2004.00233.x.

Alexander, J. C. 2006. *The Civil Sphere.* New York: Oxford University Press.

Alexander, J. C. 2013. "Struggling Over the Mode of Incorporation: Backlash against Multiculturalism in Europe." *Ethnic and Racial Studies* 36 (4): 531–556. doi:10.1080/01419870.2012.752515.

Autrey, J. 2005a. "The Fab IV." *Fort Worth Star Telegram*, May 24.

Autrey, J. 2005b. "Record Number of Women Make Semifinals." *Fort Worth Star Telegram*, May 25.

Beneito-Montagut, R. 2011. "Ethnography Goes Online: Towards a User-Centred Methodology to Research Interpersonal Communication on the Internet." *Qualitative Research* 11 (6): 716–735. doi:10.1177/1468794111413368.

Born, G., and D. Hesmondhalgh, eds. 2000. *Western Music and Its Others: Difference, Representation, and Appropriation in Music.* Ewing, NJ: University of California Press.

Cantrell, S. 2005. "Chinese Pianists Strong Players in Cliburn This Year." *Dallas Morning News*, May 17.

Dayan, D., and E. Katz. 1992. *Media Events: The Live Broadcasting of History.* Cambridge, MA: Harvard University Press.

Delanty, G. 2011. "Conclusion: On the Cultural Significance of Arts Festivals." In *Festivals and the Cultural Public Sphere*, edited by L. Giorgi, M. Sassatelli, and G. Delanty, 190–198. New York: Routledge.

Duchen, J. 2009. "The Murky Music Prize." *The Independent*, April 21.

English, J. F. 2011. "Festivals and the Geography of Culture: African Cinema in the 'World Space' of Its Public." In *Festivals and the Cultural Public Sphere*, edited by L. Giorgi, M. Sassatelli, and G. Delanty, 63–78. Abingdon: Routledge.

Gay, W. L. 2005. "Cliburn's Feminine Tone: Female Artists Dominate Once Macho Piano Contest." *Chicago Tribune*, March 9.

Glick Schiller, N., T. Darieva, and S. Gruner-Domic. 2011. "Defining Cosmopolitan Sociability in a Transnational Age. An Introduction." *Ethnic and Racial Studies* 34 (3): 399–418. doi:10.1080/01419870.2011.533781.

Hennion, A. 2001. "Music Lovers: Taste as Performance." *Theory, Culture & Society* 18 (5): 1–22. doi:10.1177/02632760122051940.

Johnson, M. 2009. "The Dark Side of Piano Competitions." *The New York Times*, August 7.

Kraus, R. C. 1989. *Pianos and Politics in China: Middle-Class Ambitions and the Struggle over Western Music.* Cary, NC: Oxford University Press.

Mangan, T. 2009. "Blind Pianist Shares Top Van Cliburn Prize." *Orange County Register*, June 12.

Marton, A. 2009. "Where are all the Russians?" *Fort Worth Star-Telegram*, May 17, p. AA05.

McCormick, L. Forthcoming. *Performing Civility: International Competitions in Classical Music.*

N.A. 2013. "Notes and Noise." *The Economist.*

BOOKS, BODIES AND BRONZES

Nash, K. 2008. "Global Citizenship as Show Business: The Cultural Politics of Make Poverty History." *Media, Culture & Society* 30: 167–181. doi:10.1177/0163443707086859.

Potter, J. 2002. "Two Kinds of Natural." *Discourse Studies* 4 (4): 539–542. doi:10.1177/1461445602004004001.

Ritterman, J. 2002. "On Teaching Performance." In *Musical Performance: A Guide to Understanding,* edited by J. Rink, 75–88. Cambridge: Cambridge University Press.

Sassatelli, M. 2011. "Urban Festivals and the Cultural Public Sphere: Cosmopolitanism between Ethics and Aesthetics." In *Festivals and the Cultural Public Sphere,* edited by L. Giorgi, M. Sassatelli, and G. Delanty, 12–28. Abingdon: Routledge.

Schütz, A. 1951. "Making Music Together: A Study in Social Relationship." *Social Research* 18: 76–97.

Simmel, G. 1971. *On Individuality and Social Forms: Selected Writings.* Chicago: University of Chicago Press.

Yang, M. 2007. "East Meets West in the Concert Hall: Asians and Classical Music in the Century of Imperialism, Post-Colonialism, and Multiculturalism." *Asian Music* 38 (1): 1–30. doi:10.1353/amu.2007.0025.

Zeeble, B. 2009. "Asian Pianists Sweep Van Cliburn Competition." *Voice of America News,* June 9.

Index